2024

MEDICARE
MADE 123EASY

Facts you need to know

A non-government resource

by David and Ian Schaeffer

Medicare Made 123Easy

The author may be contacted at the following address:
American Retirement Advisors
8501 E Princess Drive Suite #210
Scottsdale, AZ 85255
Phone: 877-220-1089 Web sites: AmericanRetire.com, 123EasyMedicare.com, 123EasyWorkshops.com

Cover Graphic, Cover Design, and Page Design by Ian M. Schaeffer

Initial Printing, August 2012, Second Edition, January 2013, Third Edition, January 2014, Fourth Edition, January 2015, Fifth Edition, January 2016, Sixth Edition, January 2017, Seventh Edition, January 2018, Eighth Edition, January 2019, Ninth Edition, January 2020, Tenth Edition, January 2021, Eleventh Edition, March 2024

Schaeffer, David P. & Schaeffer, Ian M.
Medicare Made 123Easy: Facts you need to know / David and Ian Schaeffer

ISBN 978-1-304-58503-5

FOREWORD

"Just as I told you in 2011, when you wrote the first copy, I remain very "high" on this book. Not only does it explain Medicare and Medicare Supplement Insurance well, it does it in language so simple…"

Kevin Michael Lynch
MBA, CFP®, CLU®, ChFC®, RHU, REBC, CASL®, CAP®, LUTCF, FSS

Assistant Professor of Insurance; Charles J. Zimmerman Chair in Insurance Education at The American College of Financial Services

LEGAL DISCLAIMER AND TERMS OF USE

This book is for educational purposes only. All the web pages and images are copyrighted by the original owners. This book is not connected with or endorsed by the U.S. government or the federal Medicare program.

You do not have resell rights or giveaway rights to any portion of this publication. Only customers who have purchased this publication are authorized to view it. This publication contains material protected by federal copyright laws. No part of this publication may be transmitted or reproduced in anyway without the author's prior written permission. Violations of this copyright will be enforced to the full extent of the law.

The information, services, and resources provided in this book are based on the current environment at the time of printing. The process presented has been successful for countless beneficiaries. That being said, the Medicare space is constantly changing; the sites and services described in this book may change, cease, or expand with time. We hope that the principles taught remain evergreen. However, we cannot be held responsible for changes that may affect the outcome or applicability of the techniques presented.

Any examples are based on our own estimates and are only generalized figures of what one could expect at any given point in the pages presented.

Screenshots in this book are from publicly available sources. All product names, logos, and artwork are copyrights of their respective owners. None of the owners have sponsored or endorsed this publication. While all attempts have been made to verify the information provided, the authors assume no responsibility for errors, omissions, or contrary interpretations of the subject matter herein. Any perceived slights of people or organizations are unintentional. The purchaser or reader of this publication assumes responsibility for the use of these materials and information. The author reserves the rights to make changes and assumes no responsibility or liability whatsoever on behalf of any purchaser or reader of these materials.

American Retirement Advisors and its affiliated entities are privately owned and operated. This book, "Medicare Made 123Easy," is a non-government resource. If you are looking for the official Medicare website, please visit www.Medicare.gov. CMS, the Centers for Medicare and Medicaid Services, has rules and regulations that we must follow when discussing Medicare Advantage and Prescription Drug Plans. This book will only cover general information about Original Medicare, Medicare Advantage, Medicare Supplements, and Prescription Drug Plans as everyone's needs are different. If you are interested in specific information about specific products, please request insurance company-created product information approved by the department of insurance in your state.

DEDICATION

To Thea (mom) and Lora, who've been the rock-solid anchors for my wild ideas. Your relentless quest to keep things clear and your knack for steering my passions in the right direction have been the secret sauce of this book's journey. It's through your plain-talk and no-nonsense approach that these pages have come to life.

Table of Contents

Appendices

Introduction

By David P. Schaeffer

Sally: "Hey, honey. Look, we got another email from Super Duper Insurance Company. They even included an interactive guide this time."

John: "I know… and a dozen notifications on my phone too!"

Sally: "Well, shouldn't we do something about it?"

John: "I would, but with all the information out there - digital enrollment guides, health plan comparison apps, provider networks, and everything from Medicare Part A to Part D, Medicare Advantage, Medigap, and my HR department telling me something completely different than what I see on Medicare's own website… It's overwhelming!"

I know from experience this is the reality for most folks reading this book. Perhaps that's why you picked it up, or maybe you're just keen to understand the evolving world of Medicare. Whatever your reason, I'm delighted you're here! We're about to make this whole process 1-2-3 Easy.

I've sifted through numerous guides, been to countless "webinars" and downloaded a whole ream of paper worth of "self-help booklets" promising to demystify Medicare, only to find biased information and sales pitches for one insurance company or another. It's frustrating… at least it was for me.

The truth is, Medicare is not one-size-fits-all. It's a landscape continuously shaped by policy changes, technological advancements, and evolving healthcare necessities.

I've listened to many clients express their confusion and stress about navigating Medicare... In the 10 years since I first published this book, and the 20 years helping folks before that… the story hasn't changed all that much.

This drove me to contribute something genuinely helpful and why I realized the key to understanding Medicare didn't lie in complexity, but in simplicity. That's where "123Easy" comes in. We all crave simplicity, from choosing a quick meal on the go to planning for retirement. Why should understanding Medicare be any different?

Welcome to "1-2-3 Easy" - the guiding principle of this book, and the mantra of our practice. With the assistance of our cartoon influencer turned senior advocate, Easy Eddie®, we'll walk you through the Medicare landscape step-by-step, and answer all the questions we could think of to write in this book along the way. You'll meet Easy Eddie® soon; he's got some great tips up his virtual sleeve.

Think of this book as your guidebook for Medicare no matter what your situation. My aim is to clarify each option, backed by the latest resources and tools available in 2024.

We'll break down complex government terms into our own translation which we have coined 'Medi-care-eeze'™. We will debunk common misconceptions, and provide a clear, step-by-step guide to navigate Medicare—from applying for Original Medicare (Parts A and B) to choosing the plan or plans that best suit your needs all the way to how "agents" are compensated.

By the end of this book, you'll not only understand what Medicare is, but also, how to ask the right questions to the right people as you make your Medicare decisions as easy as counting to three.

So, if you're ready to turn this complex maze into a straightforward path, let's get started!

~ *David P. Schaeffer*, *CEO of American Retirement Advisors, and founder of 123EasyMedicare*

Chapter One:
Getting Started

"Starting your Medicare adventure is a lot like setting off on a road trip. First things first - you have to know where you're kicking off from. It's about understanding your current healthcare landscape, your needs, and the coverage you've got. That's your starting line. From there, we can map out the best route to get you cruising smoothly into your Medicare years."

So, where to begin?

Your Medicare journey can start from any number of places. You could be turning 65, still working, and have incredible group health insurance. You could be turning 65, not covered under group health insurance, and counting the seconds until you are eligible for Medicare. Or, you could be over 65, planning to retire, and will be losing that group health insurance. It is important to identify what your starting point is, so you understand what choices you have.

Important Note: Enrolling in Social Security and Medicare are separate events. You do not need to enroll in Social Security to begin your Medicare.

Here are your starting points:

1 **Turning 65, still working, covered under group health insurance**

2 **Turning 65, not covered under group health insurance**

3 **Over 65, losing group health insurance**

If your starting point is #1, **turning 65, still working, covered under group health insurance**, you might be thinking "Do I need to do anything?"

The answer is… it depends. If your plan is 'creditable' you have the option to "DO NOTHING." If the answer is no, it is not creditable, then you are going to really be starting at #2 and must enroll in Medicare to avoid penalties.

To determine if you need to do anything, you need to verify if your current insurance plan is considered "creditable." Here is our first Medi-care-eeze™ term. Medicare defines creditable coverage as coverage that is "at least as good as what Medicare provides."

To find out if your current plan is deemed 'creditable' ask your Human Resources department for an "Evidence of Coverage" for the plan you are on. In that evidence of coverage document, you would search for the words "Notice of Creditability." This will tell you if your plan provides coverage that Medicare deems 'creditable'.

Once you confirm that your coverage is, in-fact, 'creditable' then you can breathe a sigh of relief, as you now officially have the choice to "do nothing" you can delay your enrollment in

Parts A and B of Medicare and suffer no penalties or loss of options.

If your plan is not deemed 'creditable' then you must enroll in Medicare, as technically, you will not be covered by your group insurance in the eyes of Medicare when you later go to enroll.

With a Retiree plan you may need to get Parts A and B of Medicare, to go with it.

If your starting point is #2, **turning 65, not covered under group health insurance,** then you must enroll in Medicare to avoid any late enrollment penalties.

If your starting point is #3, **over 65, losing group health insurance,** you are the same as #2, only we need to make sure you don't fall for the COBRA offer.

COBRA *is not considered creditable coverage by Medicare!* If you are Medicare eligible and elect COBRA after you are eligible for Medicare or are on COBRA once you become eligible for Medicare (turning 65) and do not enroll in Part B and D of Medicare, you will experience a lifetime penalty for every month that you did not have creditable coverage. This penalty will be applied to your premium for both Medicare Part B and Part D once you do enroll in an eligible plan and will not go away.

Warning for folks still working!

For those of you that are still working, you will most likely engage your trusted Human Resources (HR) department or benefits coordinator for help. This is where you have comfortably received healthcare guidance for years. We get it... even so, you must be aware, that your HR partner is not a Medicare expert. Medicare is much different than an employee plan. And, while they are trying to help, they do not always know the intricacies of Medicare, and often give incorrect or incomplete advice.

For example:

HR will likely tell you to run out and get Part "A" because its "free." They will try and explain that Medicare will coordinate with your existing health coverage... (fun fact, it is not that simple, and often leads to more work and confusion for both you and the doctor's office, with no additional coverage, just more headache). In their minds, they are advising you to "get more coverage at no cost." They are just trying to help... they just don't know what they do not know.

Some challenges... If you enroll in Part A of Medicare, you are no longer able to contribute to a Health Savings Account (HSA) without penalty. You are also deemed ineligible for many manufacturer coupons for those pricey medications (yikes). You also now added a layer of difficulty with a "primary" and "secondary" payor that is now involved in getting your medical expenses paid.

HR may also suggest that you transition to Medicare when you turn 65, even if you have the option of remaining on your group health insurance. Just note, that it is illegal for HR to force you to enroll in Medicare. In order to make the determination of whether or not this transition is in your best interest, not just theirs, we have developed what we call the "Stay or Go Analysis™."

This process is designed to compare the cost of your insurance at work to the costs associated with each of your Medicare plan options. Sometimes, the math shows Medicare is a more cost-effective option, but not always! In our practice we find it flushes out to about 80% making the transition, 20% staying on their employer plans while working.

We are going to go in-depth with how to do this analysis, and ultimately how to line up all your options on a single sheet of paper. More on this in a couple chapters.

So… what happens if you do not enroll in Medicare when you are eligible?

Here is a quick breakdown sourced from Medicare.gov:
Every month you delay enrolling in Part B of Medicare outside of your initial enrollment period, you will pay a penalty of 10% for every 12-month period you delay. At the same time, you are also incurring a penalty on Part D, this penalty is calculated by multiplying 1% of the national base beneficiary premium (NBBP), by the number of months you were without Part D coverage. In 2024 that NBBP is $34.70. This number changes annually.

To drive the point home, imagine for a second that you put off enrolling in Part B and Part D for 12 months after you're eligible, and you don't have any other coverage that counts during this time. Here's the scoop:

For Part B: This delay means your monthly premium will go up. Since the Part B penalty is 10% for each full 12-month period you wait, and you've delayed for a bit over a year, you're looking at a 10% increase in your Part B premium. (In 2024, that would be $174.70 + 10% = $191.51)

For Part D: It's similar but a bit different in calculation. Your penalty is 1% of the national base beneficiary premium, which is $34.70 in 2024, for each month you didn't sign up. So, after 12 months, you'd have an extra 12% added on. That's roughly an additional $3.47 to your monthly Part D premium. Premiums for Part D plans range from $0 to just under $200 depending on where you are in the country.

Both these extra amounts become part of your regular monthly payments for as long as you have Part B and Part D, meaning these are lifelong penalties.

We want to make sure you avoid these at all costs!

AVOID PENALTIES AT ALL COSTS!

Chapter Two:
The Parts of Medicare

"Slicing through the layers of Medicare is like crafting a classic dish, beginning with the essential ingredients. Part A lays the hearty base, Part B infuses the flavor, and from there, we garnish with the choice of supplements or Advantage plans to complete a personalized menu of coverage that satisfies every palate."

Let's start with **Original Medicare**, which consists of Parts A and B. This is the foundation of your Medicare coverage.

Part A

Part A primarily covers hospital stays, skilled nursing facility care, hospice care, and some home health care. Think of it as your safety net for big-ticket items in healthcare after a per-occurrence deductible of $1,632 in 2024.

Hospital Stays: When you're admitted to the hospital, Part A kicks in. It covers your room, meals, general nursing, drugs as part of your inpatient treatment, and other hospital services and supplies.

Skilled Nursing Facility (SNF) Care: If you need specialized nursing care after a hospital stay (like physical therapy and rehab), Medicare Part A covers it, in a Medicare-approved facility for a limited number of days. But remember, to qualify for a SNF you must have been in the hospital for at least three consecutive days, excluding the day you are admitted, and the day you are discharged and classified as in-patient, unless you qualify for a Medicare-approved SNF 3-day Rule Waiver.

Hospice Care: For those with a terminal illness, Part A provides care to make you more comfortable. It includes things like medical equipment, pain management, emotional, and even spiritual support.

Home Health Care: Part A may cover some skilled nursing care, as well as physical therapy, speech-language pathology services, or continued occupational services. This one gets a lot of folks confused. This is only care that is deemed medically necessary by a medical professional and ordered by a doctor for a specified period of time.

Home health care is NOT custodial care (also known as daily living care, things like bathing and dressing) nor is it long-term care.

Premium for Medicare Part A

For most folks, if you or your spouse of 10 years or more have been working for 40 quarters (10 years of full-time work) in the United States, you have already been paying into Medicare. Therefore, there is usually no charge for Medicare Part A. (You already paid for it through that pesky Medicare tax taken out of your paycheck).

Now, let's say that you are not "most folks", and have <u>not</u> earned your full 40 quarters to have Part A covered completely… There are ways to still get Part A covered.

According to CMS.gov for 2024, if you have earned at least 30 quarters (you can check your quarters earned at https://www.ssa.gov/myaccount/), or married to someone with at least 30 quarters, you may be charged a reduced monthly premium of $278 per month.

If you have earned less than 30 quarters, for instance, and you were in a tax-exempt position, you would be responsible to pay the full premium for Part A, which is $505 per month in 2024.

Part B

Part B covers a variety of outpatient medical services including doctor visits, preventive services, and medical supplies.

Doctor Visits and Outpatient Services: Part B is there for you when you visit a doctor for either a routine check-up or a specialist consultation.

Preventive Services: As we all hear every day, preventive care is key, and Part B covers many such services, like flu shots and cancer screenings. (To see complete list visit https://www.medicare.gov/coverage/preventive-screening-services.)

Durable Medical Equipment (DME): Need a wheelchair or a walker? Typically, Part B helps cover these with a 20% copay.

Other Services: Part B also covers things like ambulance services, mental health care, and some outpatient prescription drugs (mainly those you can't administer yourself).

Premium for Medicare Part B

Monthly Premium: Unlike Part A, Part B comes with a standard base monthly premium of $174.70 in 2024.

If you are a "high-income earner" you will incur a surcharge on your Parts B and D of Medicare. **This is not a penalty!** The Income-Related Monthly Adjustment Amount (IRMAA) is based on your Modified Adjusted Gross Income (MAGI) looking back at your tax returns from 2 years ago.

Example: If we are in the year 2024, your IRMAA determination would be based on your MAGI from 2022. If your income then drops back down in 2023, then in 2025, this surcharge will go away automatically.

I have included a chart showing the income thresholds for 2024 on the next page. If your income drops due to some "change of life event" there is a form you can submit to have this surcharge removed or reduced. It is the form labeled SSA-44, and can be found here: https://www.ssa.gov/forms/ssa-44.pdf.

Annual Deductible and Coinsurance in addition to your monthly Part B premium: There's an annual deductible ($240 in 2024), and after you meet it, you typically pay 20% of the Medicare-approved amount for most doctor services.

IRMAA* Rates for Medicare Beneficiaries

2024

income-related monthly adjustment amount

Beneficiaries who file individual tax returns with income: Individual	Beneficiaries who file joint tax returns with income: Married	IRMAA PART B	Total monthly Part B	IRMAA* PART D	Total Part's A & B + Surcharges
$103,000 or less	$206,000 or less	$0.00	$174.70	$0.00	$174.70
above $103,000 up to $129,000	above $206,000 up to $258,000	$69.90	$244.60	$12.90	$257.50
above $129,000 up to $161,000	above $258,000 up to $322,000	$174.70	$349.40	$33.30	$382.70
above $161,000 up to $193,000	above $322,000 up to $386,000	$279.50	$454.20	$53.80	$508.00
above $193,000 and less than $500,000	above $386,000 and less than $750,000	$384.30	$559.00	$74.20	$633.20
$500,000 or above	$750,000 and above	$419.30	$594.00	$81.00	$675.00

Source: CMS.gov https://www.cms.gov/newsroom/fact-sheets/2024-medicare-parts-b-premiums-and-deductibles#:~:text=The%20annual%20deductible%20for%2

Review of Original Medicare – A tasty example

Think of Original Medicare as your classic, no-frills pie on the dinner menu. It's made up of two main ingredients: Part A (Hospital Insurance) and Part B (Medical Insurance).

 Medicare Part A - The pie crust: Just as a pie needs a good crust to hold everything together, Medicare Part A forms the base of your healthcare coverage. It covers your hospital stays, skilled nursing facility care, rehab, hospice care, and some aspects of home health care. It's your foundation, essential and sturdy.

Medicare Part B - The filling: Now, what's a pie without its filling? Part B adds to Part A, covering necessary medical services like doctor visits, outpatient care, preventive services, and some home health care. It's the foundation of your pie, filled with the essential healthcare services you might need.

Together, they offer comprehensive coverage. But before you dig in, remember that this pie isn't all-inclusive. **There's no coverage for the prescription drugs you take at home, and you might find yourself paying for each service with deductibles and 20% coinsurance after Medicare pays its share**.

Here are two major risks of enrolling in only Medicare Part A and Part B (Original Medicare):

1) Absence of Out-of-Pocket Maximums

Unlike many private insurance plans, Original Medicare doesn't cap your annual spending.

There's no out-of-pocket maximum, which means if you have a year with significant health issues, your share of covered services could add up quickly, with no limit to cap those out-of-pocket expenses. You can imagine how expensive that could quickly get if you have ever been to the hospital for a night and seen the bill… imagine paying 20% of that.

2) No Prescription Drug Coverage

Medicare Part B covers certain outpatient prescription drugs, typically those administered in a doctor's office or a hospital outpatient setting. However, most prescriptions you take at home aren't covered. This gap can be a significant oversight, as these out-of-pocket medication costs can add up even faster than a 20% hospital stay if not managed correctly.

How about an example.

Example with Original Medicare – New Hip

Hypothetically, the doctor says you need to get a hip replacement. Now let's say hip replacement is going to cost $40,000 if you were to pay cash.

Here is a quick table breaking down YOUR cost for that example hip replacement…

Your initial bill is $40,000. Part A will pay its portion (after you pay an initial deductible of $1,632). Part B will pay its portion (after you pay its $240 deductible). Now, Parts A and B will pay up to 80%, leaving your responsibility as the leftover 20%, in addition to your deductibles. **You are responsible for about $9,872 of that bill.** I have included a chart here for you visual learners out there.

EXAMPLE: NEW HIP WITH ORIGINAL MEDICARE			
Initial Bill	**$40,000**	With Parts A and B Only	
Cost Paid by each Part of Medicare	<u>Part A</u> Coverage	<u>Part B</u> Coverage	<u>You Pay</u>
Deductible	$1,632	$240	$1,872
Coinsurance	20%		$8,000
	Your out-of-pocket cost:		**$9,872**
*You must also factor in your monthly premiums, not accounted for here in this example			

I do not know about you… but having to pay $9,872 out-of-pocket for a single procedure is not something that I want to be on the hook for… neither does anyone else.

So, what do you do.

That is why there are so many plan options to augment your coverage. Plans like you have very likely seen on TV, read a pamphlet for, or even watched a seminar about. Let me show you what these plans are, so you can understand how folks get that $9,872 down almost nothing.

Medigap (Supplement)

Just as a topping completes a pie, Medigap policies are designed to "fill in the gaps" of Original Medicare. These federally standardized plans, labeled A through N, ensure that no matter where you buy your plan, the coverage remains the same - though service may differ. It's like ensuring every bite of your pie is just right, without any missing flavors, regardless of which pie shop you decide to visit.

Federally Standardized Plans: Plan G often tops the popularity charts because it offers comprehensive coverage. In 2024, once you meet the Part B deductible of $240, Plan G takes care of any additional Medicare-approved expenses for the rest of the year. You won't face copayments or coinsurance for medical services; your only ongoing cost is the monthly premium. Example, that $9,872 bill we just talked about, would be no more than $240, plus the cost of your premiums for the plan. This makes budgeting for healthcare costs more predictable, even if you need extensive treatment or see multiple specialists. With Plan G, once you've paid your deductible and premiums, your Medigap policy handles the rest.

Even if you get diagnosed with "heebie-jeebies" and require significant amounts of medical attention and frequent visits to different specialists across the country, your out-of-pocket costs are covered at $0, after your premiums, and that small annual deductible.

Back to the hip replacement example, let's add in a Medigap Plan G to supplement your Original Medicare. Medicare will pay their portion (80% minus the deductibles) and Medicare will bill the supplement (Plan G) the remainder (20%). If this is our first medical expense of the calendar year, you simply pay the Part B deductible, your premiums, and don't worry about any additional costs.

EXAMPLE: NEW HIP WITH ORIGINAL MEDICARE + MEDIGAP PLAN G			
Initial Bill	$40,000	Parts A and B + Medigap Plan G	
Cost paid by each part of Medicare	Part A Coverage	Part B Coverage	What You Pay
Deductible	$1,632 (Plan G covers this)	$240	$240
Coinsurance	(20% x $40,000) = $8,000 (Plan G covers this)		$0
	Your out-of-pocket cost:		$240
*You must also factor in your monthly premiums, not accounted for here in this example			

Now this math looks a lot more appetizing, don't you agree?

Medigap is a separate policy: Keep in mind, Medigap is not part of Original Medicare. It's a separate insurance policy you buy from a private company to cover the costs that Original Medicare doesn't. Even though these policies are sold by different insurers, they are federally standardized, which means the coverage is identical across companies. For instance, whether you buy Plan G from Company XYZ or Company RST, you'll get the same medical benefits. The only difference will be the premium you pay. This standardization ensures that regardless of the insurer, your Plan G benefits remain consistent—like getting the same reliable pie from different bakeries.

EXCEPTIONS: If you live in **Minnesota**, **Wisconsin**, or **Massachusetts**, you have special Medicare Supplement plans available. They are similar, but different to what is available in the other 47 states. **Why?** In 1992, the National Association of Insurance Commissioners (NAIC) established standardized Medigap plans (Plans A-J) to offer consistent coverage and easier comparison across states. However, these three states opted out of full standardization and maintained their own existing Medigap plan structures.

Freedom of Choice: With Medigap, you can visit any doctor or hospital that has an active license to practice medicine. Much like being able to enjoy your pie at any spot of your choosing, there are no network restrictions, offering you the freedom to savor your coverage anywhere in the United States of America.

<u>(Okay, put on a snarky accent in your head for a second)</u>

Have you ever heard this one, *"You can't go to that doctor, they don't take Medicare!"*

It is super common, and one remark that we inevitably get to debunk at each workshop we host, and in almost every meeting we have with clients.

Let's dig in, shall we?

There are 3 different classifications of doctors according to Medicare.

1) Participating Provider (98%):
These doctors have agreed to accept Medicare's payment rates for covered services... in English, if Medicare says they will pay a doctor $100 for a visit, participating providers agree to see you for that $100. This group accounts for 98% of practicing providers in the United States according to the latest 2024 participation report posted on CMS.gov.

2) Non-participating Provider (1.1%):
These doctors haven't agreed to accept Medicare's payment rates...in English, let's pretend Medicare says they will pay a

doctor $100 for a visit, non-participating providers might say "No, our visits cost $120." With Original Medicare Parts A and B, you would be stuck paying that difference of $20 in addition to your 20% of the payment for that visit.

With Original Medicare and a Supplement Plan G, however, those excess charges would be picked up by that Medigap Plan. If you have already satisfied your annual Part B deductible, this means you would pay nothing for that visit - just your premiums.

This is often where you run into issues where offices do not want to submit the paperwork to get paid by Medicare... so they put that on you to get it done.

If you are ever put in that situation, here is the form you need to download from Medicare, <u>CMS-1490S</u>.

You simply pay the provider, then submit this form, Medicare will send you a check for their portion of the bill, and the supplement will send you a check for their portion, leaving you fully reimbursed. (Remember the Part B deductible, $240 in 2024, must still be paid one time each calendar year). This group accounts for about 1.1% of providers.

3) Opt-out Provider (<1%):

This group accounts for less than 1% of all providers in the United States. These doctors have chosen to not accept Medicare at all. These are the tricky ones. These are often called "concierge physicians." These providers charge anywhere between $5,000 to $10,000 on average per patient per year to have direct access to their services. While Medicare will not pick up that annual fee, if that doctor sent you for labs, diagnostics, or referred you to a participating specialist, those charges would all be picked up by Medicare and your supplement. So, you still have a green light to go to them with a Medigap, it just might cost you more upfront to satisfy their fee.

Still with me?

To sum it up. With Original Medicare and a Medicare Supplement, you can see **Any Doctor, Any Hospital, Anywhere in the USA.** With Medicare and a Medicare Supplement (Plan G specifically) you can go regardless of the type of physician. With Medicare and a Medicare Supplement, you go to the doctor, the doctor or you submits the bill to Medicare (Medicare is your insurance company), then Medicare electronically notifies your Medigap company of the remainder of the bill. Your Medigap plan pays its portion, and you are left with whatever cost remains after that depending on your plan letter.

At the core, with a Medicare Supplement (Medigap), what you need to remember is that **Medicare is your insurance company**.

We will talk about the other Medigap Plan letters like Plan N when I teach you how to go shopping later in this book.

But wait!
One more very important piece regarding Medigap plans.

No Prescription Drug Coverage: Medigap plans do not cover prescription drugs. Nor does Original Medicare Parts A or B. You will need to add a prescription drug plan to go along with your Original Medicare and Medigap plan, regardless of which letter you select.

That necessary prescription drug coverage is called Part D.

Let's talk about that next.

Part D

Medicare Part D is the part of Medicare that covers prescription drugs. It's provided through private insurance plans approved by Medicare. Each Part D plan has its own list of covered drugs (formulary), with different premiums and cost-sharing structures.

Formulary: Each plan covers a specific list of prescription drugs. While plans can vary in which drugs are covered, all Part D plans must cover <u>all</u> drugs in the following categories: HIV/AIDS treatments, Antidepressants, Antipsychotic medications, Immunosuppressants, Anticonvulsants, Antiemetics, and at least two drugs in all remaining categories.

Pharmacy Network: Your Part D plan usually has a network of pharmacies where you can get your medications. Even though you can technically go to any pharmacy in the United States, the cost of your medications will depend on whether the pharmacy is in your plan's network.

Most plans have two types of pharmacies in their network: preferred pharmacies and standard pharmacies. Preferred pharmacies typically have lower costs for your covered medications.

Tiers: Drugs on a plan's formulary are grouped into tiers, and each tier has a different cost. Generally, lower tiers cost less, while higher tiers (like specialty drugs) cost more. These can vary from plan to plan. Some plans may cover a medication at tier 4, while others consider it a tier 3. Once again it is important to do your research before you enroll. (We will teach you how later in the book).

Costs: Your out-of-pocket costs for Part D include a monthly premium, a yearly deductible (although not all plans have one), and copayments or coinsurance for each prescription. These costs vary by plan.

An important heads-up. Diving into Part D without mentioning the Late Enrollment Penalty would be like skipping the fine print… If you delay enrolling in Part D after you're first eligible and don't have other 'creditable' prescription drug coverage, you may face a late enrollment penalty. This penalty is added to your monthly Part D premium, potentially for as long as you have Medicare prescription drug coverage. **Yes, even if you do not take any prescription medications**, Medicare does not care. You still must have Part D coverage to avoid this penalty. We will dig into the specifics and how to avoid this penalty in a later chapter, so stay tuned for more on this critical topic.

Back to the main points.

Coverage Phases of Part D: Part D coverage has several phases, each with different cost-sharing rules:

Deductible Phase: You pay the full cost of your drugs until you meet the plan's annual deductible. These deductibles range anywhere from $0 to $545 in 2024.

Initial Coverage Phase: After meeting the deductible, you pay a copayment or coinsurance for each prescription until your total drug costs reach the initial coverage limit of $5,030 in 2024, set by Medicare.

Coverage Gap (Donut Hole): Once your total drug costs exceed the initial coverage limit, you're in the coverage gap. In this phase, you'll pay a percentage of the cost for generic and brand-name drugs until your retail costs reach $8,000 in 2024, the threshold to qualify for catastrophic coverage.

Catastrophic Coverage: After reaching the out-of-pocket threshold of $8,000, you enter catastrophic coverage. In this phase, you pay zero for covered drugs for the rest of the year.

I am going to provide a detailed example and even a chart on how these phases work when we get into shopping for a plan, so stay tuned.

What about extra help for folks that need financial assistance to pay for some very costly medications? For individuals with limited income and resources, Medicare offers a lifeline known as the Part-D Low Income Subsidy. This program helps with paying for Medicare prescription drug program costs like premiums, deductibles, and coinsurance. While this book is not going to get into the details of this program, understanding it exists is beneficial. For more information about the Extra Help program and eligibility criteria, visit Medicare's official help page https://www.medicare.gov/basics/costs/help/drug-costs.

Review

Let's review the Medicare menu so far.

Original Medicare, including Parts A and B, lay the foundation. Part A is your hospital coverage, while Part B takes care of medical services after you meet an annual deductible, leaving you typically, with 20% of costs to pay. There's no cap on what you can spend out-of-pocket with just Original Medicare all by itself, hence the popularity of a Medigap policy to step in and cover those gaps. Part D is the essential, but not required cherry on top, covering prescriptions—but watch out for that late enrollment penalty if you delay signing up without other qualifying coverage.

This is not the end of the menu though, there is one more item to add. We talked about Medicare Part A and B being a pie, with Medicare Supplements being the icing, and Part D being the cherry on top... but what if you don't like pie? What if you wanted a cake instead?

Maybe you have noticed some clever TV spots, heard about some ridiculously enticing benefits on the radio, quickly scrolled through smiling senior faces on social media, and maybe just maybe you clicked on one of those ads, to notice they are trying to sell you a Medicare Advantage plan... for this analogy, we are going to call Medicare Advantage plans "cake."

Why?

Because with a Medicare Advantage plan, instead of Medicare being your insurance company, you assign your Medicare benefits to a third-party insurance company. So, it's like you have the same coverage as Original Medicare, but instead of Medicare paying the bills, your insurance company now handles that for you. You still pay your Medicare Part A and B premiums, but Medicare has in essence offloaded the responsibility of managing your healthcare to a company of your choosing. In exchange, these companies are incentivized to provide high quality care, reduced costs, and improved outcomes in just about any way they see fit. Medicare pays the Advantage Plan companies more, the higher their quality of care, and patient outcomes are. Often this means offering a plethora of "free non-Medicare covered extras."

It is important to note: Going this route, while you will still pay for your Medicare Part A and B premiums, Medicare will no longer be your insurance company. If you choose this dessert, you're agreeing to let a private plan take over the serving duties from Medicare itself, with different rules to follow.

Alright, let's slice into the details of Medicare Advantage plans next.

Part C - Medicare Advantage

Part C, also known as Medicare Advantage plans, are an alternative way to get your Medicare Part A and Part B coverage. These plans are offered by private insurance companies approved by Medicare. They bundle Part A (hospital insurance) and Part B (medical insurance), and most include Part D (prescription drug coverage) as well. These function very similar to the group, and individual health care plans most of us have had all our lives. To be clear, when you select a

Medicare Advantage plan, Medicare is no longer your insurance company; you are transferring your benefits to a particular Advantage plan in exchange for its coverage, and often additional non-Medicare included extras provided by a particular plan.

Compliance notes: Medicare, also known as, the Centers for Medicare and Medicaid Services (CMS) no longer allows us to name the potential additional benefits that are often included with these plans. So, in place of the names of the benefits, we will be using symbols to represent them. They did not say anything about using pictures!

Key Features of Medicare Advantage Plans:
All-in-one coverage. These plans typically wrap in Parts A, B, and D as well as include extra benefits not covered by Original Medicare, like 👀, 👂, 🦷, 😁, 🛒, 🛏, even 💵 back and a maximum-out-of-pocket, capping the amount of money you are responsible to pay out of pocket for medical expenses in a calendar year, excluding prescription drugs.

You may have heard from the same family and friends that told you a certain doctor "doesn't take Medicare", that advantage plans are limited to very small local networks of providers that you can see... I am here to tell you that is not the case in most instances. Here are the different types of Medicare Advantage plans, each with their own unique way of managing costs to provide you access to the highest quality care they can.

Different Types of Medicare Advantage Plans: There are several types of Medicare Advantage plans, including Health Maintenance Organization (HMO) plans, National HMOs, Preferred Provider Organization (PPO) plans, Private Fee-for-Service (PFFS) plans, as well as Medicare Saving Accounts (MSA). Each type has different rules for how you receive services (like whether you need a referral to see a specialist or if you must use doctors in the plan's network). Here are those different plan types explained as sourced from Medicare.gov.

Health Maintenance Organization (HMO)
Requires getting care from doctors, providers, and hospitals in the plan's network (except for emergency, urgent care, or out-of-area dialysis). Some HMOs may allow out-of-network services for a higher cost. Very few plans still require referrals to see specialists. Important to note here for shopping later: In 2024 there are many HMOs that have opened their national networks, allowing you to receive routine care anywhere in the country, not just in your immediate service area. For instance, if you have a house in two different states, the original answer used to be "Get a PPO, or a Medicare Supplement

(Medigap)"… now, you have the ability on some of these Medicare Advantage plans to remain in-network across the country.

Preferred Provider Organization (PPO)

Offers networks of doctors, providers, and hospitals. You pay less for using in-network providers. You can use out-of-network providers for covered services, usually at a higher cost. No need for a primary care doctor or referrals to see specialists. Be careful here, even though the plan might pay for an out-of-network doctor, there are still networks associated with PPO plans; it is important to research your doctors before just enrolling in a PPO, thinking you are covered. The provider must still accept the plan's payment.

Medicare Savings Account (MSA)

Combines a high-deductible health plan with a medical savings account. You can use the funds in the MSA to pay for Medicare-covered costs. No network restrictions: you can see any Medicare-approved provider. Doesn't include drug coverage; you need a separate Part D plan.

Private Fee-for-Service (PFFS)

The plan determines payment amounts for services and how much you pay. You can go to any Medicare-approved provider that accepts the plan's terms. May or may not offer drug coverage; if not, you can join a separate Part D plan.

Costs: Costs vary among Medicare Advantage plans. Typically, there is no premium for these plans above and beyond the Medicare Part B premium. Unlike a Medigap plan, Advantage plans are all about copayments or coinsurance for covered services. We will get into these costs when we talk about shopping, as there are a lot of them to research as you get into the details of each individual plan.

But first, a quick review of what we know to this point.

Review

We know now that **Original Medicare** includes Parts A and B. We know that **Part A** only helps to cover things associated with hospital stays. **Part B** helps with medical necessities after an annual deductible. Original Medicare leaves you open to 20% of your medical expenses. To cover that 20% you have options.

One of those options is selecting a Medicare Supplement (Medigap plan, likely a Plan G) and a Part D prescription drug plan to go with it.

The other option is to transfer your benefits to an Advantage plan that often wraps your Part A, B and D into a single plan, and functions like the individual and employee plans that you are already accustomed to. While Medicare is no longer your insurance company, if you select an Advantage plan, you get access to all the same covered services Original Medicare has to offer, as well as access to additional benefits like ●●, ♥, ⚕, ⚕, 🚗, so long as you stay within a given care network.

Now, with an exasperated tone, you might be saying…
"Great… with all that, I think I am even more confused… now how am I supposed to pick what is right for me?"

My response… stick with me! And don't go thinking you should just ask your neighbor or Uncle Bob that "knows all about this stuff."

The right answer for you, could be a different answer for your neighbor, or even your spouse in the same house!

This leads us to Chapter 3, shopping. We are going to take all of that information you now have about the pieces of Medicare, and put that to work finding a plan or plans that make sense based on what you need out of your healthcare coverage.

Chapter Three:
Shopping

Supplement Plans | Prescription Drug Plans | Advantage Plans

"Embarking on your Medicare journey shouldn't be like finding your way through a maze. Consider this chapter your trusty GPS, guiding you through the landscape of Medicare choices. We'll lay out a roadmap to navigate the complexities of premiums, benefits, and costs — turning the twists and turns of Medicare into a straight path forward. With a clear comparison and a sprinkle of sage advice, making informed decisions about your healthcare in retirement will be as easy as pie — be it apple or chocolate!"

The Shopper's Guide:

Navigating the sea of Medicare options can feel daunting but worry not — we've got the perfect compass to guide you through. As we embark on this shopping journey, let's lay the groundwork: you'll need to have your Original Medicare (Parts A and B) in place. It is the essential base, whether you're topping it off with a Medigap policy or opting for a Medicare Advantage plan — like deciding between a classic apple pie or a molten chocolate cake.

To help you compare your options side-by-side and make an informed decision, we've crafted a simplified version of the tool used daily by our Certified Medicare Planners®. This straightforward guide will become your high-level map, charting the course through premiums, benefits, and costs. It's designed to clarify the differences at-a-glance, making your comparison shopping 123Easy.

Here is the base of the Shopper's Guide. If you want to follow along through this chapter, go ahead and grab a piece of paper and something to write with. Start by making a chart just like the one you see here. We will be adding more rows to the bottom, so make sure to give yourself plenty of room on the page.

SHOPPER'S GUIDE				
	Group Health Ins.	Original Medicare	Medicare Supplement	Medicare Advantage
Plan Premium				
...	...	...	...	...

In the coming pages, we'll fill in this grid together. You'll learn how to personalize it with the numbers and features that matter most to you. By the end, you'll be able to weigh the pros and cons of each option with confidence.

For those with 'creditable' coverage available through an employer, it's time to pull out your plan's Summary of Benefits.

You'll need to figure out the premium you're responsible for, whether it's deducted from your paycheck weekly or bi-weekly and convert this figure into a monthly premium, so it aligns with the monthly format we'll use in our comparison grid. If you have a Retiree plan through your previous employer, not an employee plan, you will need to write down your premiums for

Part A and B as well as your plan premium through your previous employer.

While you are at it, you might as well include the premiums associated with Original Medicare too, as you now know what those are for 2024.

Jot down these premiums in the appropriate cell of the grid and set aside the rest of your benefits information for now.

SHOPPER'S GUIDE				
	Group Health Ins.	Original Medicare	Medicare Supplement	Medicare Advantage
Plan Premium	$_____	Not Applicable		
Medicare **Part A***	Only if Retiree	$0		
Medicare **Part B**	Only if Retiree	$174.70		

*Numbers in the chart are for reference only. Actual costs will vary and are subject to change.

Next, we'll navigate the waters of Medigap plans, also called Medicare Supplements. Thanks to their federal standardization, finding the right Medigap plan can be straightforward once you know what you're looking for. Let's begin by exploring the array of Medigap plans, from A through N, and find the one that fits your needs like a glove.

First things first, let me show you all the Medigap Plan letters (A-N). A larger version of this chart can be found in Appendix D.

Medigap Plans *(Issued after January 1, 2020)* *If Medicare eligible after 2019* **Medigap Plans A Through N**

Medigap policies (including Medicare Select) can only be sold in twelve standardized plans. This chart gives you a quick look at all the Medigap plans and their benefits. Read down to find out what benefits are in each plan. If you need more information call your State Insurance Department.

A	B	D	G (High Deductible)	K	L	M	N	C (Only available if you were age 65 before 1/1/2020)	F (High Deductible)	F
Basic Benefits, including 100% Part B co-Insurance	Basic Benefits, Including 100% Part B co-insurance	Basic Benefits, Including 100% Part B co-insurance	Basic Benefits, Including 100% Part B co-insurance	Basic Benefits, Including 100% Part B co-insurance After $2,800 deductible is reached	Basic Benefits, including 100% Part B co-insurance	Hospital and preventative care paid at 100%; other Benefits paid at 50%	Hospital and preventative care paid at 100%; other Benefits paid at 75%	Basic Benefits, including 100% Part B Co-Insurance. You pay up to $20 copay for office visit, up to $50 copay ER	Basic Benefits, Including 100% Part B co-insurance	Basic Benefits, Including 100% Part B co-insurance After $2,800 deductible is reached
		100% Skilled Nursing Coinsurance	100% Skilled Nursing Coinsurance	100% Skilled Nursing Coinsurance After $2,800 deductible is reached	50% Skilled Nursing Coinsurance	75% Skilled Nursing Coinsurance	100% Skilled Nursing Coinsurance	100% Skilled Nursing Coinsurance	100% Skilled Nursing Coinsurance	100% Skilled Nursing Coinsurance After $2,800 deductible is reached
	100% Medicare Part A Deductible	100% Medicare Part A Deductible	100% Medicare Part A Deductible	100% Medicare Part A Deductible After $2,800 deductible is reached	50% Medicare Part A Deductible	75% Medicare Part A Deductible	50% Medicare Part A Deductible	100% Medicare Part A Deductible	100% Medicare Part A Deductible	100% Medicare Part A Deductible After $2,800 deductible is reached
				100% Medicare Part B Deductible After $2,800 deductible is reached					100% Medicare Part B Deductible	100% Medicare Part B Excess Charges	100% Medicare Part B Deductible After $2,800 deductible is reached
			100% Medicare Part B Excess Charges	100% Medicare Part B Excess Charges After $2,800 deductible is reached					100% Medicare Part B Excess Charges	100% Medicare Part B Excess Charges After $2,800 deductible is reached
	80% Foreign Travel Emergency	80% Foreign Travel Emergency	80% Foreign Travel Emergency	80% Foreign Travel Emergency After $2,800 deductible is reached			80% Foreign Travel Emergency	80% Foreign Travel Emergency	80% Foreign Travel Emergency	80% Foreign Travel Emergency After $2,800 deductible is reached	80% Foreign Travel Emergency
				Out-of-pocket limit $7,060; paid at 100% after limit reached	Out-of-pocket limit $3,530; paid at 100% after limit reached					

Medigap Plans C, F and High Deductible are only available if you were age 65 or Medicare eligible before 1/1/2020.
Plan N pays 100% of the Part B coinsurance, except for a copayment of up to $20 for some office visits and up to a $50 copayment for emergency room visits that don't result in inpatient admission.

Above is the grid without any modifications so you can see the choices available.

In our experience when looking at this chart, it does more to confuse folks than help, so we went in and shaded all the coverage gaps that exist with each plan letter. If you notice, Plan G, results in the most comprehensive coverage, filling all the gaps aside from the annual Part B deductible.

This is why, when choosing to go the Medicare Supplement route, a Plan G is the most popular choice.

Medigap Plans *(Issued after January 1, 2020)   If Medicare eligible after 2019*   Medigap Plans A Through N

Medigap policies (including Medicare Select) can only be sold in twelve standardized plans. This chart gives you a quick look at all the Medigap plans and their benefits. Read down to find out what benefits are in each plan. If you need more information call your State insurance Department.

A	B	D	G	G High Deductible	K	L	M	N	C	F High Deductible	F
											Only available if you were age 65 before 1/1/2020
Basic Benefits, including 100% Part B co-insurance	Basic Benefits, including 100% Part B co-insurance	Basic Benefits, including 100% Part B co-insurance	Basic Benefits, including 100% Part B co-insurance	Basic Benefits, including 100% Part B co-insurance After $2,800 deductible is reached	Basic Benefits, including 100% Part B co-insurance	Hospital and preventative care paid at 100%; other Benefits paid at 50%	Hospital and preventative care paid at 100%; other Benefits paid at 75%	Basic Benefits, including 100% Part B Co-insurance. You pay up to $20 copay for office visit, up to $50 copay ER	Basic Benefits, including 100% Part B co-insurance	Basic Benefits, including 100% Part B co-insurance After $2,800 deductible is reached	Basic Benefits, including 100% Part B co-insurance
		100% Skilled Nursing Coinsurance	100% Skilled Nursing Coinsurance	100% Skilled Nursing Coinsurance After $2,800 deductible is reached	50% Skilled Nursing Coinsurance	75% Skilled Nursing Coinsurance	100% Skilled Nursing Coinsurance	100% Skilled Nursing Coinsurance	100% Skilled Nursing Coinsurance	100% Skilled Nursing After $2,800 deductible is reached	100% Skilled Nursing Coinsurance
	100% Medicare Part A Deductible	100% Medicare Part A Deductible	100% Medicare Part A Deductible	100% Medicare Part A Deductible After $2,800 deductible is reached	50% Medicare Part A Deductible	75% Medicare Part A Deductible	50% Medicare Part A Deductible	100% Medicare Part A Deductible	100% Medicare Part A Deductible	100% Medicare Part A Deductible After $2,800 deductible is reached	100% Medicare Part A Deductible
				100% Medicare Part B Deductible After $2,800 deductible is reached					100% Medicare Part B Deductible	100% Medicare Part B Deductible After $2,800 deductible is reached	100% Medicare Part B Deductible
NOT COVERED	NOT COVERED	NOT COVERED	100% Medicare Part B Excess Charges	100% Medicare Part B Excess Charges After $2,800 deductible is reached	NOT COVERED	NOT COVERED	NOT COVERED	NOT COVERED		100% Medicare Part B Excess Charges After $2,800 deductible is reached	100% Medicare Part B Excess Charges
NOT COVERED	NOT COVERED	80% Foreign Travel Emergency	80% Foreign Travel Emergency	80% Foreign Travel Emergency After $2,800 deductible is reached	NOT COVERED	NOT COVERED	80% Foreign Travel Emergency	80% Foreign Travel Emergency	80% Foreign Travel Emergency	80% Foreign Travel Emergency After $2,800 deductible is reached	80% Foreign Travel Emergency
					Out-of-pocket limit $7,060; paid at 100% after limit reached	Out-of-pocket limit $3,530; paid at 100% after limit reached					

2024 2 MEDICARE Supplement Plan Compare 01.10.2024

Medigap Plans C, F and High Deductible are only available if you were age 65 or Medicare eligible before 1/1/2020.
Plan N pays 100% of the Part B coinsurance, except for a copayment of up to $20 for some office visits and up to a $50 copayment for emergency room visits that don't result in inpatient admission.

NOTE: Plan F did not "go-away." If you were eligible for a Plan F prior to 1/1/2020, you can get a Plan F. For folks that became eligible after 1/1/2020, a Plan F is not an option for you.

Since Medigap coverage is federally standardized, the benefits are consistent across all insurance companies offering these plans. The only difference is the premium you will pay, which varies based on the following factors, your **age**, **gender**, **zip code**, and **tobacco use**.

You will find, if you search enough unique zip codes (like our advisors do every day) there are over 200 different insurance companies, and sub-companies offering Medicare Supplement plans across the country.

> **Note:** During your initial enrollment period, which we'll explore in Chapter 4, you won't face medical underwriting, making this an ideal time to enroll, especially if you have existing health issues.

How To Shop for a Medigap:

Our Certified Medicare Planners® subscribe to an actuarial service that pulls the rates from every company in a geographic area, even those that are only offered to private groups (think the ones with three letters in a row that also help tow your car if you get stuck). This allows us to have a complete picture of the marketplace, not just a limited view from any one quote tool. The only way to get accurate pricing without such an actuarial tool or using a Certified Medicare Planner® is to search Medicare.gov for every company offering the particular plan letter you wish to shop for, then going to each of their individual company-sponsored websites to get a quote.

I include a screen-by-screen tutorial of how to access the shopping tool on Medicare.gov in the appendix of the book.

IMPORTANT: It doesn't matter which company you buy from, whose insurance company logo is on your Medigap card, or what you are paying for a monthly premium! A Medigap Plan from Company A is exactly the same as a Medigap Plan from Company B.

You can pick the lowest cost plan and add that dollar amount to the premium section under Medigap, in your Shopper's Guide and move on.

But you did not pick up this book to get the basic answer… you picked up this book to learn from the experts.

When selecting a Medigap plan, the hidden details can make all the difference.

Let's consider how a Certified Medicare Planner® or a savvy shopper like yourself would approach this after getting the premiums from every company available in the market for the given Medigap plan letter you wish to shop for:

Rate History: Investigate the rate history of the top ten lowest-cost plans. When did they last increase or decrease their premiums? This historical data can give you insights into potential future costs.

Corporate Rating: Assess the corporate ratings of these companies. These ratings act as a performance report card, indicating how well a company has managed to pay Medicare claims over time.

Marketplace Longevity: It's prudent to prioritize companies with at least a five-year track record in your market. While the coverage itself remains identical regardless of the company, longevity can signal stability—reducing the likelihood you'll need to switch plans due to a company exiting the market.

While it's entirely possible to carry out this research on your own, remember that agents and brokers are not allowed to charge for their services. Seeking out guidance from a knowledgeable professional, who can navigate the intricate details and offer a complete market overview, can prove invaluable. Whether it's through one of our Certified Medicare Planners® or a trusted local advisor, ensure they are licensed and have a comprehensive portfolio of plans for your area. The right expertise can simplify this process, providing you with confidence in your decision; the wrong advice could cost you thousands of dollars in premium.

Now, let's reconnect with our Shopper's Guide.

After sifting through the options and pinpointing the Medigap plan that best suit your criteria—considering premium affordability and the insurer's reliability—it's time to fill in the blanks.

You can pick any Medigap letter that suits your needs, but for example purposes in this book I am going to use Plan G.

Take the monthly premium of the chosen Medigap plan, which you've identified as offering the best value for your age, gender, zip code, and smoking preference, then enter it in the 'Medicare Supplement' column of your grid.

As you document the premium for your selected Medigap plan in the Shopper's Guide it's also an opportune moment for those with employer coverage to bring out your Summary of Benefits. Examine the details, particularly the deductible you're responsible for, and record this in the "Group Health Ins." column of your grid.

	Group Health Ins.	Original Medicare	Medicare Supplement (Plan G)	Medicare Advantage
SHOPPER'S GUIDE				
Plan Premium	$_____	Not Applicable	$_____	
Medicare **Part A***	Only if Retiree	$0	$0	
Medicare **Part B**	Only if Retiree	$174.70	$174.70	
Plan Deductible	$_____	Not Applicable	$0	
Part A Deductible	Only if Retiree	$1,632	$0	
Part B Deductible		$240	$240	

*Numbers in the chart are for reference only. Actual costs will vary and are subject to change.

In the Shopper's Guide, you'll notice I have pre-filled some numbers for you. These figures represent the Medicare Part A and Part B deductibles, which are standard amounts you would pay annually for services under Original Medicare. For Part A, the deductible is $1,632, covering your hospital services, and for Part B, it is $240, which applies to medical services.

Including these deductibles in the grid provides a clearer picture of the out-of-pocket costs you're responsible for before insurance kicks in.

Going back to our Plan G example, this plan covers the Part A deductible entirely and leaves you with the Part B deductible to pay. This is why you'll see the Part B deductible listed in the Medigap column.

One of the great benefits of a Medigap Plan G is how it streamlines your healthcare expenses. Regardless of the number of medical visits or hospital stays you have within a calendar year, your out-of-pocket cost is capped. Once you've paid your monthly premium and met the annual Part B deductible, Plan G covers the rest of your Medicare-approved medical costs for the year.

It is that straightforward — no unexpected bills for covered services. Before we pivot from the simplicity of Medigap to the diverse landscape of Medicare Advantage plans, we need to remember to add into the Shopper's Guide a Part D prescription drug plan to go with your Medigap plan.

Let's cover those before moving on.

Selecting a Part D

As we have already discussed, Original Medicare (Parts A and B) DO NOT include drug coverage. You must enroll in a stand-alone Part D, or part of a drug plan incorporated into a Medicare Advantage plan to have coverage and to avoid any Medicare-imposed penalties.

The process of selecting the most appropriate Medicare Part D prescription drug plan is straightforward once you understand the components, and phases that make up the federally standardized Part D coverage. Let's begin by separating Medicare Part D into the four phases.

Phase 1 *The Deductible*

Under Medicare's standard model, a Part D prescription drug plan may include a deductible of up to $545 for 2024. If the plan indeed does have a deductible, you must pay it completely before you receive any benefits. Some plans may have a deductible only on brand and specialty drugs or certain drug tiers. It all depends.

Phase 2 *The Initial Coverage Limit*

This is $5,030 for 2024. Essentially, this is the amount of coverage you initially receive in exchange for your premium. In English, this is the initial pool of benefit money in your plan. To reach this initial coverage amount, subtract the plan's negotiated retail price of the prescriptions from the pool of benefit money until the benefit money pool is empty. Once you've used the initial coverage limit, we move to the coverage gap (the donut hole).

Phase 3 *The Coverage Gap (aka The Donut hole)*

This part gets a bit sticky, so hang in there. We need to get from $5,030 retail cost spent on your behalf to $8,000. That is the coverage gap. In the coverage gap, you pay 25% of the retail cost of a non-generic prescription. The prescription drug plan pays a portion, and the manufacturer of the drug pays their portion. This takes place until all parties have spent a total of $8,000 on prescriptions drugs.

Phase 4 *Catastrophic Coverage*

Once you reach the catastrophic coverage section you pay nothing for covered medications. Covered medications will vary from plan to plan, so it is important to do your research. Below is a simplified example of the math that goes along with a list of medications that would cost about $3,250 for the year, and how this person would experience each phase of Part D coverage.

To shop for these you have a few choices. To start, you can simply go to Medicare.gov and follow the prompts. Enter your medication list and search for all the prescription drug plans in your area and start digging into each one that pops up on the list for the various coverage components. Alternatively, you can go to each one of the insurance company web sites, type in the same list of medications, and see the pricing directly on the company's website… or, realistically, you can give a Certified Medicare Planner® a call, schedule a 60-minute appointment, and we can go over all of your choices and even throw it into a comparison chart just like the one I've been explaining for you to use at home. Like I said... you have choices and picking a Part D is straightforward, and **probably one of the easiest things to shop for once you know what you are looking at.**

Here is an example. If I am searching for a Part D plan and am taking a medication that has a retail cost of $2,000 every month, my goal would be to find a plan that would get that potentially $24,000 annual medication cost down as low as possible.

Let's say that I find a plan, using Medicare's plan finder that says it will cover my prescription for an estimated annual cost of only $3,250. Just looking at the difference between $24,000 and $3,250, I know that I am excited! But what goes into that estimated annual cost?

Again, just an example, but here would be how a plan could break down in each phase. If the plan has a monthly premium of $10. I know that I will need to pay that every month no matter what. Now, my medication is an expensive one at $2,000 retail cost and I also have a deductible on this plan of $200. I know that I will need to pay that too.

So far with this plan, I know that I will need to pay $10 for the premium and the $200 deductible. Okay, that is $210 so far.

Now I need to see what my copay is for my medication. Not the retail cost, but the cost that I am responsible for. In this example let's say my copay is $460.

So, $10 premium plus $200 deductible plus my copay of $460, means that in the first month I can expect to pay $670 at the pharmacy for my medication. This would be starting your **Initial Coverage Phase**.

Moving to the next month. Since I have completely paid my deductible, I do not need to worry about that. I know the retail cost of my medication has not exceeded the $5,030 to push me into the next coverage phase, so all I need to worry about in month two would be my premium ($10) and the copay for my medication ($460).

Into month three, things are a little trickier, as I know that my retail cost is going to now go over the edge into the coverage gap. Not by much though! Only the difference in cost. So, in this example, my exposure into the gap coverage is only $7 for month three; that is all the additional expense I would expect on top of my premium and copay.

When we get to month four, we are fully over the hill into the coverage gap (colloquially known as the "donut hole"). This is not necessarily a bad thing, just a temporary expense to get you closer to the next phase. I know that I will be in the coverage gap until the retail cost of my medication exceeds $8,000, so for this example I am sitting here for the next three months. The good news is 25% of the cost of my medication is still a lot less than paying retail!

Now we get to month seven! You have done it! You reached **catastrophic coverage**. Now the plan kicks in at 100% strength, and you pay nothing aside from your premium for the remainder of the year.

Pretty cool huh?

Here is what we have just explained in a visual format.

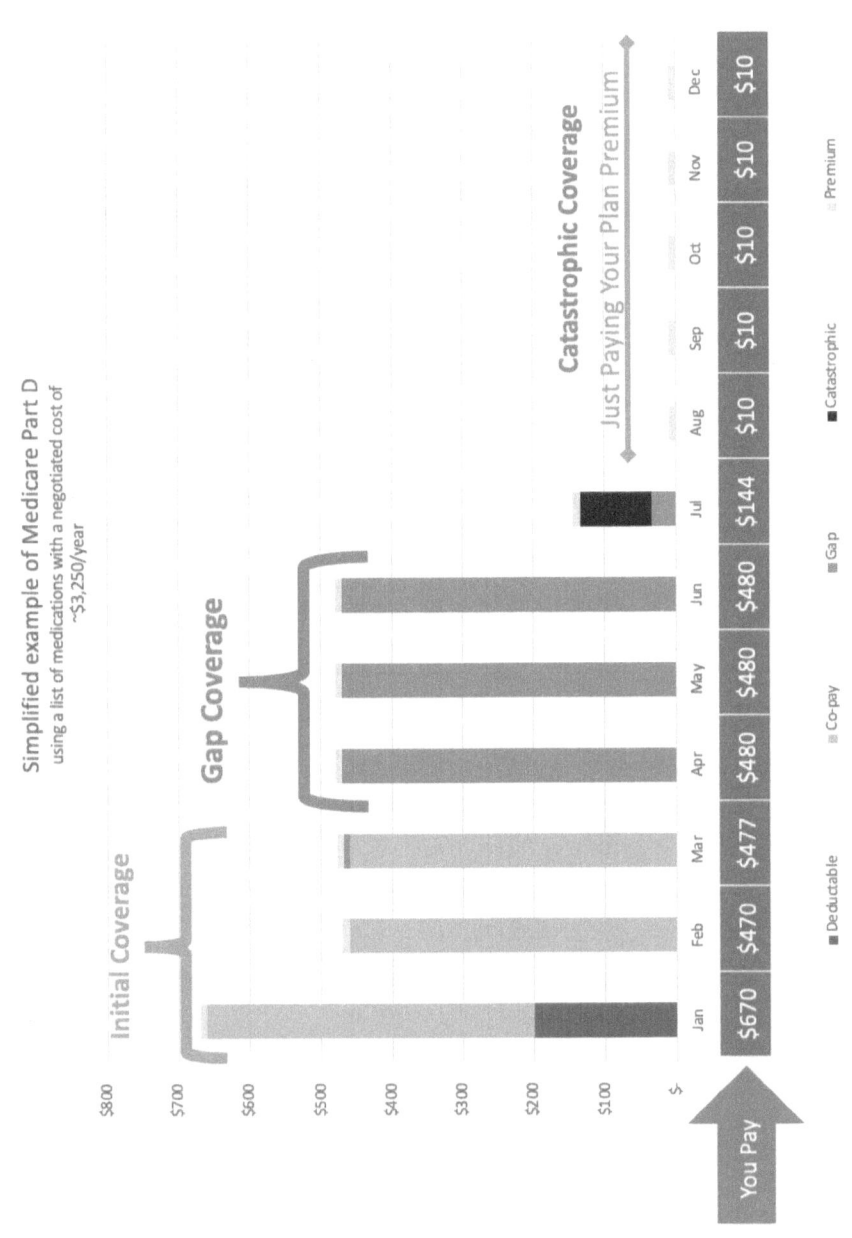

Simplified example of Medicare Part D
using a list of medications with a negotiated cost of
~$3,250/year

Initial Coverage

Gap Coverage

Catastrophic Coverage
Just Paying Your Plan Premium

	Jan	Feb	Mar	Apr	May	Jun	Jul	Aug	Sep	Oct	Nov	Dec
	$670	$470	$477	$480	$480	$480	$144	$10	$10	$10	$10	$10

You Pay

■ Deductable   ■ Co-pay   ■ Gap   ■ Catastrophic   ■ Premium

With a firm grasp of how to shop for a Medicare Supplement and what to look for when shopping for a Prescription Drug Plan, we need to update the Shopper's Guide with the plan you found that covers your medications the most appropriately.

SHOPPER'S GUIDE				
	Group Health Ins.	Original Medicare	Medicare Supplement (Plan G)	Medicare Advantage
Plan Premium	$_____	Not Applicable	$_____	
Medicare **Part A***	Only if Retiree	$0	$0	
Medicare **Part B**	Only if Retiree	$174.70	$174.70	
Plan Deductible	$_____	Not Applicable	$0	
Part A Deductible	Only if Retiree	$1,632	$0	
Part B Deductible		$240	$240	
Rx Cost (monthly estimate including premium, copays, deductibles)	$_____	$_____	$_____	

*Numbers in the chart are for reference only. Actual costs will vary and are subject to change.

When you are ready to move onto the world of Medicare Advantage plans, come on back. It does get a bit more complicated.

With Medicare Advantage plans there are a different set of factors to consider. Medicare Advantage plans, also known as Part C, package your Medicare benefits differently than a Medicare Supplement and stand-alone Part D.

These Advantage Plans often include additional perks. Yes, but with these extras come considerations like plan premiums, copayments, coinsurance, network restrictions, drug formularies, and more.

Shopping for a Medicare plan can seem quite complicated and overwhelming, but if you strip away the brand names, clever marketing, and pushy salespeople, you are left with a few basic factors to consider that will ultimately guide you to the most appropriate choice.

To navigate through these variables efficiently, we utilize another specialized tool designed by our Certified Medicare Planners®. We call this one the Medicare Advantage Plan Comparison Guide (quite original, we know). We will use this tool to get us the numbers we need to fill in the Shopper's Guide. This Medicare Advantage Plan Comparison chart helps us distill the vast array of options into a manageable selection tailored to your specific needs and preferences.

On the next page, we provide you with a snapshot of our Medicare Advantage Plan Comparison Chart. Use it as a blueprint to create one of your own or fill in the one here.

MEDICARE ADVANTAGE PLAN COMPARISON CHART						
0			Plan Name		Plan Name	Plan Name
1 Physician Name			Network 1	Network 2	Network 3	Network 3
		PCP				
		PCP				
		Cardio				
		Other				
2 Hospital						
		Other				
		Other				
3 Prescription Name						
		Dosage	/ day			
4 Preferred Pharmacy						
	Alternate Pharmacy					

Take a look at our Medicare Advantage Plan Comparison Chart. Whether it's the one on the previous page, or one you drew on your own piece of paper, this grid is designed to help you align your healthcare necessities with the offerings of various Medicare Advantage plans.

Start with preparing your grid with the information you know.

Section 1 - Physician Name: Start with a list of all the doctors that you see on a regular basis. Begin with your primary care physician (PCP) and go from there. Very important tip. Nurse Practitioners (NPs), and Physician Assistants (PAs) will not show up on most online provider directories for a given Advantage plan. You will need to find the name of the actual doctor who is responsible for the office or clinic you are visiting. Also note; dentists, optometrists, chiropractors, and naturopaths are also not likely to show up on the provider directories for individual plans. List them, but put a little note next to them; you will likely need to search the network status of these doctors in a different place – independent of the standard provider directories.

Section 2 - Hospital: If you have a preferred hospital or know of one where you would like to receive care, write it down. This is a hospital where you would receive a scheduled procedure. Emergency room visits via ambulance work a little differently, so start with just your desired hospital and we will go from there.

Section 3 - Prescription Name: Detail the medications you take, including dosages and frequency. This information is crucial for checking if your prescriptions are covered under the plan's drug formulary and what your cost might be. Be sure to check generic as well as list the brand names, as sometimes it might be more cost effective to pick up the brand (I know, sounds odd, but if you have been doing this as long as we have, you would be surprised what sort of little tricks you can pick up).

Section 4 - Preferred Pharmacy: Enter your go-to pharmacy. I would also suggest listing an alternative pharmacy you would be okay going to. Sometimes simply changing the pharmacy can make a significant difference in the cost you pay.

> **Side note:** Mail order is not always cheaper than retail pharmacies! It used to be when it first became a desirable delivery method but has since seen a major increase in cost for the convenience.

Okay, that part done, you have now set the initial requirements that must be met for a Medicare Advantage plan to make sense as an option for you.

It must cover your doctors, it must allow you to go to the hospital you desire if you were to need something done, and it must cover your prescriptions at a pharmacy you wish to pick them up at.

Next, to the fun part... finding all the information you don't know yet.

Section 0 – Plan Names: You will need to find all the Medicare Advantage plans that are available in your <u>county</u>, not necessarily zip code, as Advantage plans are usually county specific. To find a listing of all the plans available in your area, you can visit Medicare.gov. Simply click the button on the home page "<u>find health plans</u>" type in your zip-code, select your county. If there are multiple counties within your zip-code, follow the prompts, and get a complete listing of every single Medicare Advantage Plan available.

Some counties will have five to ten plans. Other places, like our headquarters in Scottsdale, Arizona (Maricopa County), have over 91 different Medicare Advantage plans to pick from. (You should see the size of the monitors we use to do this research… they are massive!). Once you have all the plans identified, list those across the top of your chart, the row labeled zero (0).

With me so far?

You should now be looking at a nice grid with your doctors, hospitals, prescriptions, and pharmacy across the left side, and then a line of the plans available to you in your area across the top.

Now, it is time to get to work researching the network status for all the providers you listed as important in the previous step.

There are several websites and "quote tools" out there that claim to be able to do this research for you, and granted, they get close, but, if you look closely, every one of those "search engines" has a disclaimer that encourages you to check the individual plan websites to determine network status. **There are no shortcuts to this process!** Taking the easy way out could lead to major disappointment and frustration later if you decide to enroll in one of these plans, and when it comes time to use it, you find that your provider no longer accepts the plan. The only place to get up-to-date provider network status is using the individual plan websites directly.

Just below all the plan names, you will need to add your doctors' names. You will then go to the provider directory for each plan on your chart and determine the provider networks associated with each specific plan.

Note: Some plans have multiple provider networks inside of them!

Yes, our Certified Medicare Planners® do this for every county across the whole country… maybe that's why half of them have lost all their hair… (ha, ha)

You might be starting to think to yourself…
 "Wow, this is a lot of work! Can't I just ask a friend or family member what plan they chose?"

We hear comments like that from folks we consult with who need our help after they selected a plan based solely on a friend's recommendation.

They then come to us asking how to correct a plan choice that lacked their doctors, lacked coverage for a particular prescription drug, and/or was missing extra benefits important to helping them maintain their healthy lifestyle.

Remember - Medicare plans are designed for individuals.

When searching for an appropriate piece of cake, you need to look for the cake that contains the ingredients that satisfy your needs.

If you have a chronic condition like diabetes, you might benefit from a cake that is sugar-free, just like a Medicare Advantage plan that caters its coverage, costs and benefits to folks managing such a condition.

There are so many options with Medicare. Don't sell yourself short by just going with what you heard advertised on TV or based on your neighbor's plan, just to make choosing easy.

You worked long and hard for the benefits you are entitled to enjoy under Medicare. If the process of choosing a plan overwhelms you, take the education you gain from this book to consult confidently with a Certified Medicare Planner®. You will better understand your options when discussing plans and they can help you narrow down your choices. **Their time is free, but their experience is priceless.**

This process is complicated. Let's walk through this again, as if a Certified Medicare Planner® was shopping for a Medicare Advantage Plan with you.

Here are the steps they follow each and every day with the clients they meet with both virtually and in their offices.

Step 1 *Identify Physicians Important to your Care*
Start with a list of all the doctors that you see on a regular basis. Begin with your primary care physician (PCP) and go from there.

> **Very important tip:** Nurse Practitioners (NPs), and Physician Assistants (PAs) will not show up on most online provider directories for a given Medicare Advantage Plan. The same goes for dentists, optometrists, chiropractors, and naturopaths.

You will need to find the name of the actual doctor who is responsible for the office or clinic you are visiting. Also note; dentists, optometrists, chiropractors, and naturopaths are also not likely to show up on the provider directories for individual plans. List them, but put a little note next to them, you will likely need to search the network status of these doctors in a different place – independent of the standard provider directories.

Step 2 *Identify Hospitals Important to your Care*
My dad is one of those guys who goes to the hospital for everything! Sometimes it may be truly necessary, other times we aren't sure if he is just going to talk to the staff; but to him,

the hospital is important. Thus, the plan he chose reflected his desire to visit a hospital he trusts to keep him healthy. If you like a place, there should be no reason you should have to leave it simply based on the coverage you select. Side note; when searching for hospitals, we are talking about in-network status routine care or scheduled procedures. If you enter a hospital via an emergency department, regardless of which Advantage Plan you select you are covered anywhere in the USA.

Step 3 *Identify Prescriptions Important to your Care*
This is the time to go grab all those pill bottles and get those handy-dandy readers on to read the exact name and dosage of each of your medications. This step is identical to what you will need to do to shop for a stand-alone Part D plan. Remember, Medicare Advantage plans simply have the Part D plan built in, but they still follow the same rules and limitations as the stand-alone Part D plans. You will want to note the pharmacy you wish to use when doing this research as pricing can vary from location to location.

Step 4 *Search Each Plan's Provider Directory*
Still have Medicare.gov open? This will be the easiest place to get access to each of the individual plan's provider directories. You can also use one of our online shopping sites https://123easy.co/providersearch.

Remember to also search for the hospital, not just the providers, while you have the provider directories open.

No matter what you do, be sure to search each **plan's network directly.** Do not ask the doctor's office "Do you take my plan?" I'm not saying that it's bad to call your doctor's office, but the people behind the desk answering the phone are not held accountable for providing you with accurate information. Most of the time it is because they are not asked the right questions. If you call and ask, "Do you take Medicare?" and they say "No", that's false! If you call the doctor and ask do you take [insert an insurance company name]?" The answer will most likely be "Yes." Great, that company may offer Group Health, Government Group Health, HMOs, PPOs, Medicare Advantage, Medicare Supplements (Plans A-N), and more. They have no idea which network, or plan, you are asking about, and they are all different! I want to make sure you know that if a provider's office takes a particular brand name, that does not mean they accept all the plans associated with that brand.

Simply put, the person on the other end of line does not know which plan you have, they cannot possibly give you an accurate answer, unless he or she knows your specific plan-ID and goes to the individual plan's network directory themselves.

To avoid all the hassles, go straight to the plan's online provider directory **first**! Then, verify with the **billing department** at the doctor's office if you do feel the need to check with your doctor's office.

For each plan network you search, put a checkbox (or if you are in the office with a Certified Medicare Planner® we will put a smiley face) indicating the doctor is covered by that plan. If they are not in, put an "X" or similar distinction showing they are not covered.

Step 5 *Choose the Plan with the Most Matches*
Now that you have a list of your doctors, and hopefully a nice grid of smiley faces and "Xs" (think B-I-N-G-O). What you are looking for is a clean line of smiley faces! This line will indicate that plan has your doctors and hospitals covered.

Step 6 *Compare Coverage and Benefits*
The most important step is complete, you have matched your doctors to the plans they are contracted with, and identified which plans allow you to go to your hospital of choice for routine and scheduled procedures. Next up, taking the short list and getting cost estimates for your medications. Using the list of plans that you narrowed your long list down to, you can go to the individual plan websites and enter your medications; every company has a tool to do this, or you can simply type your medications into the Medicare.gov tool, you used to get the list

of Medicare Advantage plans in your area. Sort plans by "Lowest drug + premium cost." Now, scroll through the list to note which plans line up to your short list, and jot down the "Total Drug & Premium Cost (for the rest of 2024)" Once you have those costs, go ahead and list them at the bottom in the corresponding columns to each of the plans.

At this point, you might find one plan offers your medications at a significantly lower cost than the rest, or you might find they are all the same.

Either way, you now have the information you need to start digging deeper into how much each of those plans are going to charge you for medical expenses. I am talking copays and coinsurance. You will need to consider costs like primary care visits, specialist visits, hospital stays, ambulance rides, labs, x-rays, etc. All plans will cover these services, but the amount you are responsible to pay can vary wildly from plan to plan.

You can do this easily using Medicare.gov by clicking the "add to compare" button, next to each of the plans on your short list you created.

At this point, you have likely narrowed down your Medicare Advantage plan search down to two, maybe three, plans that cover your doctors, hospital, prescriptions, and have reasonable copays for the medical services you care to research.

From here, let's talk about those additional "freebies" Medicare won't let me mention by name. In a lot of cases these extras are what tip people towards one plan or another.

I use the term "freebie" here loosely. **These are enhancements that can and do vary by plan.** It is important to note that not all these benefits are the same; one perk from one plan could be thousands of dollars in coverage, verses a benefit from another that could be no more than a free cleaning each year… The point is, if you know you will be needing a lot of something that might be included in one of these plans, then it would behoove you to include that need when searching for a plan.

I am talking things like , , , , . These freebies can also be found on the comparison screens using Medicare.gov. Be sure to look at the limits for each of the benefits like , and . Just because the plan "covers" these services, does not mean they cover everything, nor everywhere these services are offered. Typically, these freebies have limited networks and limited lifetime benefit amounts.

I do not know about you, but after writing this chapter I feel like I need a break, some water, and a snack before moving on... Before you grab that snack, grab your Shopper's Guide and let's fill in some more data based on your findings from your top Medicare Advantage plan choice, should you choose to go that route.

SHOPPER'S GUIDE

	Group Health Ins.	Original Medicare	Medicare Supplement (Plan G)	Medicare Advantage
Plan Premium	$_____		$_____	$_____
Medicare **Part A***	Only if Retiree	$0	$0	$0
Medicare **Part B**	Only if Retiree	$174.70	$174.70	$174.70
Plan Deductible	$_____		$0	$_____
Part A Deductible	Only if Retiree	$1,632	$0	$0
Part B Deductible		$240	$240	$0
Rx Cost	$_____	$_____	+ Part D $_____	$_____
Max-out-of-pocket	$_____	Unlimited Liability	$240 (This is only your Part B deductible)	$_____

Estimated Cost	**High** $	You use your plan to its maximum. Meaning you pay your premiums and hit your Maximum-out-of-pocket cost for the year
	Avg. $	You use your plan, see a few doctors, maybe a hospital visit. But nothing major.
	Low $	You take advantage of the "free" services, and just pay your premiums.

*Numbers in the chart are for reference only. Actual costs will vary and are subject to change.

Review

We know that shopping for a Medicare Supplement (Medigap), is straightforward. All we need to do is find an actuarial tool, or call a Certified Medicare Planner® with your **zip code**, **gender**, **age**, and if you **smoke or not**, to get a list of plans and premiums available to us. We can then use that to see with certainty our expected annual out-of-pocket costs for medical expenses.

Choosing a Part D is a recommended "must" to go along with that Medigap plan, and shopping for those is just as simple as picking a Medicare Supplement once we know what drugs we are taking and where we want to pick them up.

To compare the other option of picking a Medicare Advantage plan, we now see that it is a lot more involved than simply calling an 800 number from TV and picking from the two or three plans they offer. We need to search doctor networks, hospital networks, check copays, coinsurance amounts, prescription drug coverage, as well as maximum-out-of-pocket costs, and if the freebies being offered are even worth considering after investigating what those plans cover.

As you are starting to jot down the costs of each of your options on the Shopper's Guide, you will start to see the initial cost of a Medicare Supplement is typically higher than that of a Medicare

Advantage plan. However, it really comes down to how you use them. If you see doctors all the time, having a predictable premium and no other costs to worry about makes sense. If you never go to a doctor, and just need coverage for the occasional visit, you will know exactly what the copays and the maximum-out-of-pocket expense would be, not to mention all the freebies… it's all about choice. And you have them.

In the next chapter, I am going to break down some side-by-side comparison charts of the two major programs. Original Medicare with a Medicare Supplement and a Part D drug plan versus a Medicare Advantage plan that includes a Part D drug plan.

Chapter Four:
Let's Compare

"Medicare's two paths diverge like river and road: Supplements offer a steady, predictable current, while Advantage Plans pave a diverse route with unexpected amenities. Chart the course that mirrors your lifestyle and needs."

So far, I have shoved as much detail at you as I could think of on these pages. My goal is to give you the ability to go **out-research anyone and everyone that attempts to "sell you a plan."** You will know with certainty whether they are honest, or if they are trying to just give you what they have in their hand.

In this chapter, I want to back up a step and look at the two major programs that you can choose from to cover the unlimited liability if you were to enroll in Original Medicare (Parts A and B) all by itself.

If you already did all the work, use this to see if we are in the same ballpark as one another. If you are not, put this book down and call a Certified Medicare Planner® right now to get back in the game.

Okay, so first up. We are going to compare in my example, Medicare Supplements vs. Medicare Advantage Plans. I want to show side-by-side how the benefits work just as we do every month in our workshops. This is a slide I borrowed straight from the last show we did prior to publishing this book.

Medicare Supplement	Medicare Advantage
(Medicare + Medigap Plan G)	(Cost Plan, HMO, HMO-SNP, MSA, PPO, PFFS)
ALL Doctors **Any Doctor / Hospital in USA** *(Medigap Plan G described)*	**Network** **Doctor / Hospital** *(HMO's & HMO-SNP's Require Network, PPO's Do Not)*
NO CO-PAY *(Medigap Plan G described)*	**CO-PAY, CO-INSURANCE** *(All Medicare Advantage plans)*
$240 DEDUCTIBLE *(Medigap Plan G described)*	**$0 DEDUCTIBLE*** *(* Many plans have no deductible)*
$240 OUT OF POCKET MAXIMUM *(Medigap Plan G described)*	**OUT OF POCKET MAXIMUM** *($0 to $11,300 annually)*
Must add **a Prescription Drug Plan**	**Prescription Drug Plan** *usually* **Included**

Most popular reason plan selected
• <u>Freedom of choice</u>
  • Use any Doctor in the US
  • Use any Hospital in the US
  • No Co-Pays *(Medical Services)*
  • No Referrals required
	Most popular reason plan selected
	• <u>Low or $0 Monthly premium</u>
	  • Doctors are on Network you Select
	  • Prescriptions Benefit *(usually included)*
	  • Non-Medicare Covered Extras
	  • Simplicity of Use

Let's walk through this. On the left I am showing Medicare Supplements, on the right Medicare Advantage.

Remember with Medicare Supplements, each plan letter functions the same as any other same plan letter from any company. So, the benefits, and how they function will be the same no matter what company you purchase from. This chart is using a Plan G as its example.

Doctor Networks:

Medicare Supplement: You can go to any doctor, any hospital, anywhere in the USA.

Medicare Advantage: You must stay within the plan's network. Networks vary by plan; some are massive, some are non-exclusive, whereas others are quite small.

Copays:

Medicare Supplement (Plan G): You will have no copays for medical services.

Medicare Advantage: These plans are all about the copays and coinsurance, so it is important to complete your Medicare Advantage Comparison guide so you find the plan that minimizes these costs and allows you to maintain the care you wish to keep.

Deductibles:

Medicare Supplement: You will have a small Part B deductible annually. In 2024, this is $240.

Medicare Advantage: Most of these plans are offered with little or $0 deductible for medical expenses.

Out-of-Pocket-Maximums:

Medicare Supplement (Plan G): Since the only medical expense you have is the Part B deductible each year, that is also your out-of-pocket-maximum.

Medicare Advantage: These can range all over the place from as low as $0 to over $11,000 depending on the plan... Again, DO YOUR SHOPPING!

Prescription Drug Plans:

Medicare Supplement: You must purchase a stand-alone Part D to go along with your Medigap Plan.

Medicare Advantage: These plans typically include your Part D coverage, with some exceptions. One major exception is plans specifically designed for folks with Veteran's Administration (VA) benefits who choose to use the VA to fill their medications and do not see the need to have a drug plan since they have that reliable coverage elsewhere.

I want to share with you a similar side-by-side comparison, also straight from the last workshop that we did.

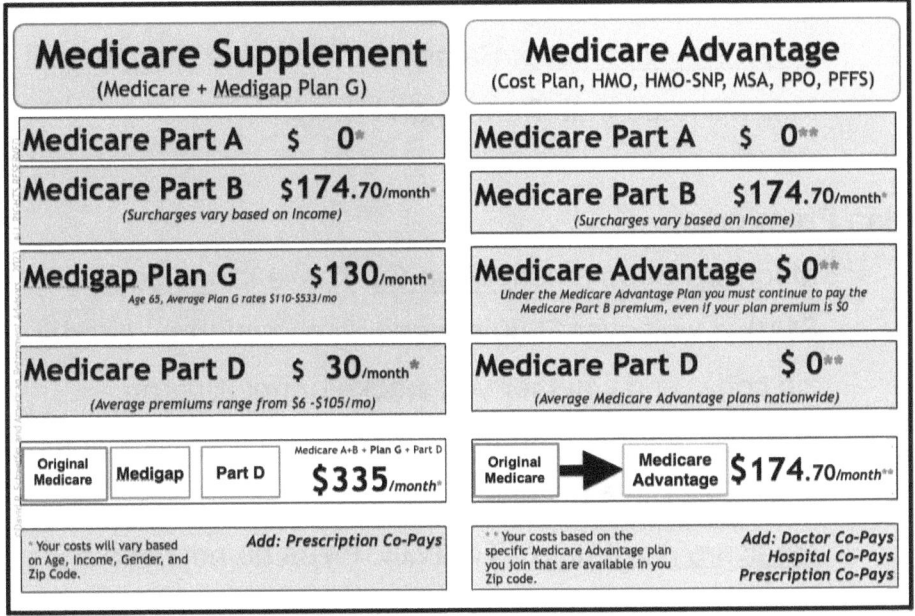

Keep in mind these are just averages. Your specific costs are going to vary depending on where you are in the country. My only intent here is to give you a rough idea of how these two programs compare.

On the left again, we have Medicare Supplements, on the right Medicare Advantage Plans.

Part A and B:

> Medicare Supplement: You will need both. Part B premium starts at the base premium of $174.70 in 2024, but can go up depending on your income (see page 28 for that IRMAA chart we talked about earlier showing the potential surcharges).
> Medicare Advantage: Same as a Medicare Supplement. You will need both Parts A and B.

Plan Premium:

> Medicare Supplement (Plan G): These range between $110 to well over $500 depending on your age, gender, zip code, and whether you smoke or not. But, on average, a Plan G premium for either a man or a woman is about $130/mo.
> Medicare Advantage: Typically, these do not have a premium above and beyond your Parts A and B of Medicare.

Part D (Prescription Drug Plan):

Medicare Supplement (Plan G): You will need to purchase a stand-alone Part D plan that covers your medications most appropriately, based on what you are taking. On average nationwide these plans are about $30 per month.

Medicare Advantage: Typically, these include a Part D plan, but do not assume it does. Make sure you check the Summary of Benefits for the plan you are considering before enrolling. We have seen some sneaky ones out there offering lots of money back; however, folks missed the fact that the plan did not include a drug plan... probably why they could afford to "give you money back."

Wrapping up:

Medicare Supplement (Plan G): You will need your Medicare A and B to go along with your Medicare Supplement, and then add a Part D plan to complete

your Medicare package, totaling three cards in your purse or wallet to take care of your healthcare needs.

<u>Medicare Advantage</u>: These are colloquially known as "all-in-one" plans as they typically wrap in your Medicare with a Prescription Drug Plan, meaning you only need to keep one card on hand to take care of your medical and prescription needs. Keep in mind though, while your Medicare Advantage plan might not have a premium, you are still responsible for paying the premium for Medicare Parts A and B.

There is no "best" answer. We don't even allow our Certified Medicare Planners® to say the word... every plan available on the market today was designed with a particular member in mind. It's your job to find the plan that was built for you!

Our Certified Medicare Planners® are trained to help.

Regardless of when you did your research, you need to keep in mind some critical dates to know when you are eligible to enroll, so you don't miss them and suffer unnecessary penalties. The next chapter is going to break down the most common enrollment periods to pay attention to.

Chapter Five:
Enrollment Periods

"It is important to act in a timely manner; but you also have to use an adequate amount of your time to choose the most appropriate plan for your needs."

When you become eligible to enroll in Medicare, it is important to act quickly; but you also have to use an adequate amount of time to choose the most appropriate option. Below is a basic breakdown of what to expect for enrollment periods. At the bottom of each page will be a visual in which each block represents a month beginning with when you are able to enroll and ending with the conclusion of the open enrollment period where applicable. For each component, Easy Eddie will provide a bit more clarity about the enrollment period.

Part A

Medicare Part A

You have an initial enrollment period (IEP) window of three months prior to, and three months after the month you turn 65. If you apply in the last three months of your initial enrollment period, your start dates will be based on your enrollment month.

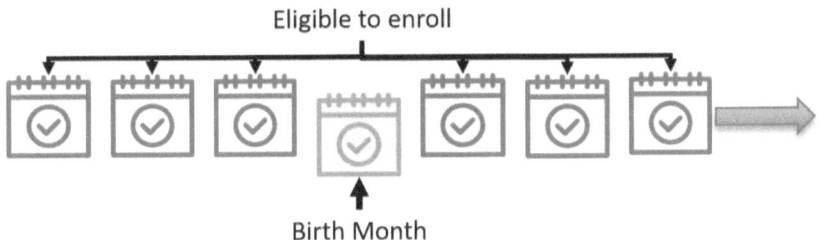

Part B

Medicare Part B

You may choose to enroll in Part B anytime three months prior and three months after your 65th birthday month (your IEP). (Most folks enroll in Medicare Parts A and B at the same time). *Exceptions apply if you are still covered by alternative 'creditable' coverage.*

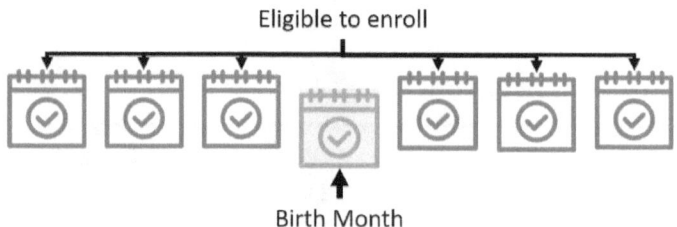

Eligible to enroll

Birth Month

Part D

Medicare Part D

You may select a Part D (Prescription Drug Plan) anytime three months prior and three months after your 65th birthday month of eligibility.

Note: There can be an <u>indefinite</u> future penalty if you do not enroll during this initial period of eligibility. Additionally, to enroll in Part D, you must have either Part A, Part B, or both. *Exceptions apply if you are still covered by alternative 'creditable' coverage.*

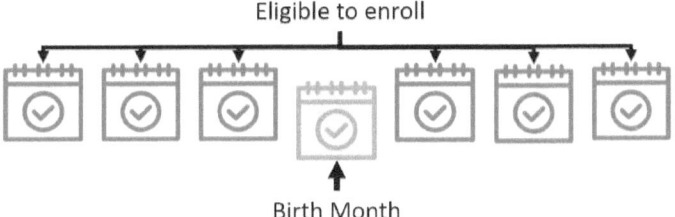

Eligible to enroll

Birth Month

Medicare Supplement (Medigap)

Medicare Supplement
(Medigap)

You have a guaranteed issue window of three months prior and six months after you turn 65 to purchase a Medigap Plan. **You are guaranteed acceptance in this time period, without any medical questions asked.**

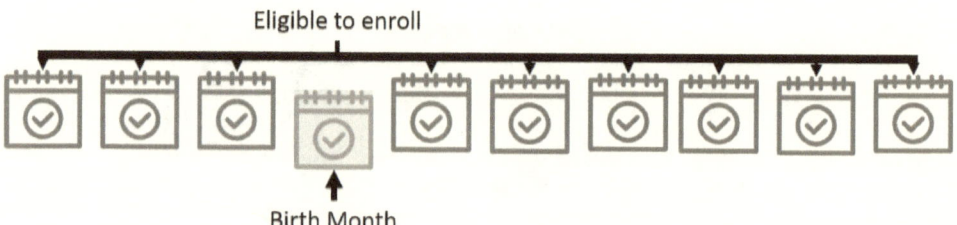

Medicare Advantage

Medicare Advantage

You have a guaranteed issue window of three months prior to, and three months after you turn 65 to purchase a Medicare Advantage Plan.

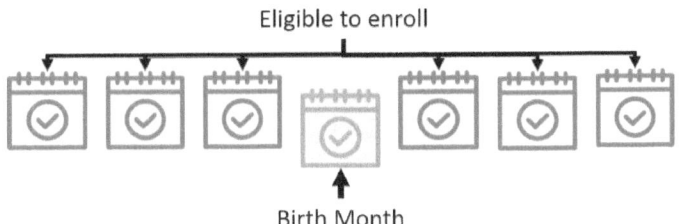

Eligible to enroll

Birth Month

Medicare Annual Election Period (AEP)

Annual Election Period
(AEP)

If you have a Medicare Advantage plan, or a Prescription Drug Plan (that goes with your Medigap), you can change that Medicare Advantage Plan or your Prescription Drug Plan **every year between October 15th and December 7th.** If you do switch your plan during this time, the new plan you select will begin January 1st of the following year. In the meantime, your previous plan will remain in effect.

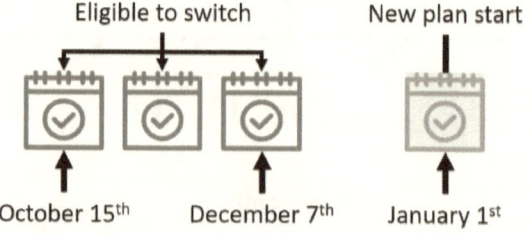

Eligible to switch

New plan start

October 15th   December 7th   January 1st

Medicare Open Enrollment Period (OEP)

Open Enrollment Period
(OEP)

If you have a Medicare Advantage plan, you are eligible for a **one-time additional change between January 1st and March 31st every year**, for a new plan effective date beginning the month following when your new plan application is submitted.

Eligible to switch

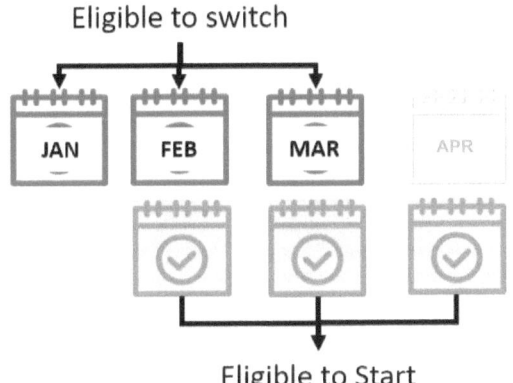

Eligible to Start

Special Enrollment Periods (SEP)

Aside from the Initial Enrollment Period surrounding someone's 65th birthday, there are some other eligibility periods that apply to more specific scenarios. These are called Special Enrollment Periods. They include early enrollment in Medicare for a disabled individual and special election periods for folks that have decided to keep working past their 65th birthday and remain on their employer provided health plan, folks that change their mind and want to change from one plan type to another, special enrollments for people that move out of a service area mid-year, and all the way to enrollment periods for designated "natural disasters." The list goes on and on.

I am going to go over a couple of the most common ones here in this chapter.

List of Common
Special Enrollment Periods

Special Enrollment Period	Description
Loss of Creditable Coverage	
Losing employer-sponsored health insurance	Enroll in Parts A & B or switch Medicare Advantage plans within 8 months of losing coverage.
Retiring with employer coverage	Enroll in Medicare within 8 months if employer stops offering Retiree health insurance.
Losing coverage under a spouse's plan	Enroll in Medicare due to divorce, death, or job loss of spouse.
Changes in Living Situation	
Moving to a new state	Switch Medicare Advantage plans if current plan isn't available in new area.
Moving into a nursing home	Switch to Medicare Advantage plan with nursing home coverage.
Changes in Eligibility	
Becoming eligible for Social Security Disability	Automatically qualify for Medicare and have SEP to choose coverage options.
Natural Disaster	Enroll in Parts A & B or switch Medicare Advantage plans if affected by a declared disaster.

*All Special Enrollment Periods are subject to change without notice from CMS, the Centers for Medicare and Medicaid Services. This list was compiled from data sourced from cms.gov 2-5-2024.

Chapter Six:
How to Enroll

Important Note: Enrolling in Social Security and Medicare are separate events. You do not need to enroll in Social Security to begin your Medicare.

"Crossing the starting line of Medicare enrollment marks a milestone. Follow these steps to transition from choice to action, turning your healthcare plans into reality."

Now let's say for this chapter that you have a firm grasp of the choices available to you, performed research on what those choices will likely cost, and have ultimately decided you are ready to enroll in Medicare.

Important Note: Medicare begins on the FIRST day of the MONTH you turn 65.

Exception: If you were born on the 1st of a month, then your Medicare CAN start the month prior. Example: If I were born on March 1st, my Medicare could start February 1st.

Great! Here is how to do it.

You can enroll in Medicare Parts A and B online at www.Medicare.gov up to 90 days before the first of the month of your 65th birthday.

Example: Your birthday is March 17th. You can enroll online any time after December 1st. Go to March 1st (first of the month you were born) and count back three months. When you enroll online, there is a confirmation screen at the end of the enrollment with a confirmation number that proves you signed up successfully. Print this for your records and your Medicare card will arrive in about three to six weeks.

Alternatively, you can visit your local Social Security office and sign up in person. Social Security offices are typically open 9:00 am - 5:00 pm M-F, but close at noon on Wednesday. You will need to go online and check the hours for the location you want to go to before making the trip. Here is a link to where to look: https://www.ssa.gov/locator/.

When signing up in person, ask for an "**Application Summary**" which is proof of enrollment in Medicare Parts A and B. Your Medicare card will arrive in three to six weeks.

Important: If you ask for a "receipt" they will say "We do not give receipts…" Ask for an Application Summary instead… it's essentially a receipt.

More choices… you can call Social Security at 1-800-772-1213 and sign up over the phone, but this is strongly discouraged. By signing up over the phone, there is no proof of enrollment like there is by doing it online or in person.

Okay, you have your Medicare Card, now what?

Enrolling in Medicare Plan(s) of choice:

Once the Medicare card arrives, enrollment in whichever Medicare Supplement and Part D Prescription Drug Plan, or Medicare Advantage Plan that is most appropriate can take place.

Chapter Seven:
Switching Plans

"Navigating the waters of Medicare doesn't mean you're anchored to one choice. Discover the ebb and flow of enrollment periods that allow you to set sail to new coverage options when the time is right."

After reviewing the eligible enrollment periods, and actually getting to the point of enrolling in the plan or plans you think are most appropriate for you, a common thought that often runs through people's minds is **"Am I stuck?"** and the true answer is both, yes, and no…

There are rules for switching after you have made your initial selection, so this is important. Making an incorrect selection when first signing up could result in you being stuck on a plan for a period.

Let me explain using some examples.

Medicare Advantage to Medicare Supplement

If you have begun your Medicare journey with a Medicare Advantage Plan, anytime during the first twelve months (known as the "trial period"), you are allowed to switch back to Original Medicare, drop the Medicare Advantage Plan, and select a Medigap and a Part D Prescription Drug Plan with no questions asked. <u>You will pay the same as anyone enrolling that month and there will be no penalties or lapse in coverage.</u>

If you select a Medicare Advantage Plan and the "trial period" has already passed, you can enroll in a Medicare supplement any month of the year if you are able to pass the medical underwriting. The challenge you face is turning off your

Medicare Advantage plan, and getting a Part D drug plan, as these two plan types have very strict enrollment periods. You can only be "released from an Advantage Plan during the Annual election Period, and select a stand along Part D plan to go with it during the "Annual Election Period" (AEP) October 15th through December 7th when you can review all next year's plans and apply to switch. Your new plan selection would be effective January 1st of the new year.

Switching from Advantage Plan to Advantage Plan

This entails no medical questions and can be done during the Annual Election Period, October 15th through December 7th, for a new plan to start January 1st of the following year. You also have one more enrollment period called "OEP" that allows for an additional one time change to another Advantage Plan between January 1st and March 31st for a new plan to start the month immediately proceeding the month of enrollment. So why switch? Some common reasons why someone would switch advantage plans include: following a doctor, getting lower cost medications, or more "extras" for the same overall cost.

Medicare Supplement to Medicare Advantage

If you have begun your Medicare journey with Original Medicare, a Medigap policy, and a Part D Prescription Drug Plan and want to switch to a Medicare Advantage Plan, you will have to wait until the Annual Election Period described above, when Advantage Plans are accepting new members for a January start. The same applies for selecting a Part D Prescription Drug Plan.

You may want to change from a Medicare Supplement to an Advantage Plan for any number of reasons; the most common reason we see is due to budget. If you find an Advantage Plan that covers your doctors, your hospitals, and your medications, with a $0 premium and a maximum-out-of-pocket that is equal to or less than your supplement premiums, it makes sense for some folks.

Switching a Part D Prescription Drug Plan

Selecting a new Part D plan follows the same rules as Advantage plans. You can shop for a new Part D, during the Annual Election Period (AEP), October 15th through December 7th and your new plan will be effective January 1st of the following year. There are no medical questions on Part D plans, you shop these plans based on the prescription medications you take on a regular basis.

Shop your Part D and Advantage plan every year. While your drug costs this year might be reasonable… The plan can change it's premiums, deductibles, co-pays and even the drugs they cover! Advantage plans change the same way but add in your doctor. Is your doctor still in your Advantage plan network next year? And if they are not where did they go? This is your opportunity to find the new network and switch so you can keep your doctor!

Switching from Medigap to Medigap

Your initial enrollment in a Medigap plan will require no medical underwriting. After that, you can change your Medigap plan any month you wish. But after your initial enrollment, switching from plan to plan, or from one insurance carrier to another, will require medical underwriting.

Chapter Eight:

Choosing an Insurance Agent or Broker

"The question isn't if you need an agent, but who will best navigate you through Medicare's myriad of choices. This chapter is your checklist for selecting an advocate who stands by your side, ensuring your Medicare experience is as easy as 1-2-3."

Do I even need an agent?

Well, the simple answer is "Yes." You are going to have to deal with a licensed insurance agent at some point in the process, no matter what. Unless you do this all by yourself online.

Whether you call the insurance company directly, dial the number for a call center you saw on television, select an independent agent or broker, or call a Certified Medicare Planner® the premiums will be the same!

The plan should pick you! The "agent" helping shouldn't be telling you which plan to select. They should serve as a guide, helping you sift through the thousands of choices to find the one that jumps to the top of the list, covering your doctors, prescriptions, and any other benefits you desire at a premium that makes sense to you.

I have developed a few key questions to ask your agent or broker before you choose to do business with them to make sure that they truly have your best interest in mind.

Questions For Your Insurance Agent/Broker

1. **Are they an agent licensed by the state in which you reside?**

   Why: If they are not licensed, technically they can't even shop for the plans in that state according to Medicare's rules and regulations.

2. **How many plans and companies do they offer? We suggest offering at least 10 different insurance companies.**

   Why: With thousands of combinations, why would you limit your research to only a select few? Why wouldn't you shop with someone like a Certified Medicare Planner® that is licensed and appointed to shop all the available plans?

3. **Do they have a bias toward one plan or another?**

   Why: If you ask someone for help and they are only contracted with two or three of the "major" carriers out there…what plans do you think they are going to present to you?

4. **Do they have a dedicated live staff (real people) to answer your questions when you need them the most?**

   Why: If you choose a friendly "local" agent who is a one-man or one-woman band, they are out selling, I mean helping nice folks like you… If you have a question in the middle of the day, do you think they will be able to stop what they are doing and take your call?

5. **How many people have they helped select a Medicare plan and are those people willing to share their experiences with you?**
Why: It is one thing to "love your agent," it is another entirely to find someone with enough clients that they have someone on just about every plan out there, to share their real-world experiences with you in regards to a plan and how it works… not just a story about the "sales process." Think about talking to someone who has been in a hospital and actually used their plan. What was their experience?

6. **Do they offer complete and comprehensive *side-by-side* comparison guides including EVERY plan in your area?**
Why: Find someone willing to complete that Shopper's Guide for you! If they are not able to provide at least as much research for you as you can do on your own, why do they deserve to earn a commission on your enrollment?

Our mission is simply to provide you with the tools and research you need to make the very best decision you can.

This is it.

I hope that after reading this book and following along with the research examples, you have a more comfortable understanding of Medicare and are ready to experience 1-2-3 Easy!

Where can you go for more information?
For more information, feel free to visit www.Medicare.gov, www.123EasyMedicare.com, www.AmericanRetire.com, or to join us at an upcoming LIVE workshop. You can get tickets at www.123EasyWorkshops.com.

Certified Medicare Planners® are available to help nationwide. Simply call 877-220-1089 and schedule an appointment to chat; we would be happy to help.

BONUS
Chapter Nine:
How agents, call centers, and the marketing companies get paid

"Medicare's landscape is dotted with signposts of choices and pathways of compensation. Understand the economic ecosystem behind your Medicare enrollment, so you can discern between guidance and persuasion in your quest for the right coverage."

If shopping with an agent is "free" how do agents get paid?

Well, the short answer is, the insurance companies pay.

The facts about "agents" and their commissions get deep and complicated quickly. It took me days to find the sources for the information I am about to share with you in this book, and I run a team of advisors...

For the agent/broker/advisor, that payment is called a commission. Commissions for Medicare Advantage Plans and Prescription Drug Plans were standardized by Medicare, back in 2008. I have included a link below for that allowable commission chart from CMS (Medicare).
https://www.cms.gov/medicare/health-drug-plans/managed-care-marketing/medicare-marketing-guidelines/agent-broker-compensation

On average, a Medicare Advantage plan, in conjunction with its affiliated insurance company is allowed to pay $611 per initial enrollment and a Part D prescription drug plan, in a similar fashion, is allowed to pay $100 per initial enrollment.

Here is a common misconception debunked...

The premium you pay for let's say a Part D prescription drug plan does not increase the amount of money that an agent gets paid!

Let's repeat that differently… If you enroll in a part D drug plan that costs $105 per month, we, as agents, get paid the same as if you enrolled in a Part D drug plan that has a premium of $10 per month!

> **We, as agents, are not incentivized at all to convince you to enroll in a more expensive plan!**

Back before these commissions were standardized, sure… it may have been the wild-wild west where the enrollments went to the companies willing to pay the most to attract the agent, and conversely, the beneficiary.

So, if we think for a second just how lucrative Medicare is, and why those call centers have the time and resources to spam you with calls, texts and emails all day, let's break down some rough numbers.

According to the US census data published for 2023, approximately 11,000 people reach the age of 65 each day. According to CMS.gov (Medicare), approximately 51% of beneficiaries are enrolled in a Medicare Advantage plan... so let's do some simple math on just that half of the population turning 65.

11,000 x 51% = 5,610 people enroll in a Medicare Advantage plan daily, that number times the maximum allowable commission is 5,610 people times $611 per enrollment = $3,427,710!

Multiplied out by 365 days, to get an annual figure of $1,251,114,150 in commissions paid per year just for Medicare Advantage premiums. Add in the average Medicare Supplement commission and Part D plan to go with that, you are looking at billions of dollars on the table. All someone needs to do is convince you, the beneficiary, to say "yes" to them...

Starting to see now, why call centers call you so frequently? Why TV commercials run non-stop? Why your mailbox is stuffed to the brim with mailers?

You can imagine there are a lot of hands in the pot fishing for the opportunity to grab even a small percentage of that available commission.

It's very important to note, that just because there is a "standard" commission, that does not mean that is what the person helping you enroll is going to get at the end of the day. There are many hands in the pot that take their cut between the insurance company paying the commission, and the person helping you to enroll.

We need to define the different types of "agents" that exist as defined by Medicare, and the associated departments of insurance across the United States, so then we can explain where they fit within even larger organizations that get paid by the insurance companies, ultimately defining where in the world all this money flows.

Independent Agents and Brokers:
- Licensed professionals who work with various insurance companies to offer a range of products, including Medicare Advantage, Medigap, and Part D plans (but not always).
- They're self-employed, representing themselves and potentially multiple insurance companies, providing comparisons and choices to beneficiaries, from the insurance companies they are licensed to represent.
- They receive commissions and other compensation from insurance companies based on enrollment activities.

Captive Agents:

- Employed directly by a single insurance company to exclusively sell their Medicare plans.
- Their focus is promoting and enrolling beneficiaries in specific plans offered by their employer.
- Like independent agents, they receive commissions and compensation tied to enrollments.

Now that we know the types of agents that are involved in the Medicare enrollment process let's break down the types of organizations that wedge themselves between the insurance companies and the agent, starting with the insurance companies themselves.

Each insurance company requires a certain minimum number of enrollments prior to granting a contract to an agent to be able to represent any one of their Medicare plan offerings. These minimums are often in the thousands, and prohibit independent insurance agents, or even small agencies from getting a direct contract to be able to sell… This is a huge problem for agencies like ours, that have a mission to get licensed and contracted with every plan in a market, so we can help you shop for every single plan, not just the very small few that will allow us to have a contract to sell...

This is where other larger agencies like Field Marketing Organizations (FMOs) come in to solve that challenge by recruiting tens of thousands of independent agents and agencies to be a part of the larger organization to meet the minimums required.

Field Marketing Organizations found a way to pool the collective enrollments of thousands of agents at any given time to meet these insurance companies-imposed contract minimums. This allowed an FMO to get licensed and contracted with just about any company they wished without concern of a minimum enrollment amount. All an agent needs to do is agree to work under that FMO and pay a marginal percentage of their current and future commissions, in exchange for this service. **It is important to know that not all FMOs represent all companies.** In fact, most only contract with the big names you see on TV. Just because the agent you go visit says they are part of a "large" FMO does not mean they can help you enroll in any plan you wish.

This is why our Certified Medicare Planners® are required to get appointed with multiple FMOs to ensure that they are truly representing as many companies and Medicare plans as compliantly possible.

There is so much more that we could get into, but I'll limit it for the sake of this book. I feel that this bonus chapter arms you with enough information to know what you are up against when it comes to choosing who can help you find the most appropriate Medicare plan for your needs.

BONUS
Chapter Ten:

Scenarios when transitioning from work to Medicare

"When life serves up a Medicare puzzle, remember, every scenario has a smart move waiting to be played."

William is about to turn 65 and is looking forward to his retirement. He's been given the green light financially to retire, and he's excited to spend more time with his spouse, who is 62 and doesn't work. One of his main concerns is ensuring his wife has continued healthcare coverage after he retires. What are his options?

Key Considerations:

Spouse's Coverage Post-Retirement: Generally, once William retires, his spouse cannot remain on his employer's health plan. This is not always the case though! Some companies offer a "bridge" program which allows their younger spouses to remain on an employer plan until they become eligible for Medicare. This would be one you would need to ask your HR department if such a program exists at your company. It is rare, but it does exist.

Spouse's Employment Status:
If William's spouse had her own employment, she could potentially get health coverage through her workplace.

Since she doesn't work, she would need to find an independent health insurance plan, through her healthcare exchange in the state they live in. However, this option can be quite expensive depending on the coverage she needs and their income.

Delaying Retirement for Coverage: Some retirees in William's situation choose to delay retirement. This way, their spouse can continue receiving health benefits under the employer's group plan until they are also eligible for Medicare.

Future Planning: When William's wife turns 65, they can explore Medicare options together to find suitable coverage for both.

Summary: William needs to consider his wife's healthcare costs when planning for retirement. Delaying retirement or enrolling in Medicare, and finding his wife an independent healthcare plan while continuing to work, are options to ensure continuous coverage for his spouse.

Scenario #2:
Enhancing Medicare Education in the Workplace

Bernadette, with 20 years as an HR Manager at a medium-sized manufacturing company, faces a challenge. She has a growing number of employees approaching retirement and is responsible for providing them with exit materials, including guidance on transitioning to Medicare. How can she effectively support her employees in making informed Medicare decisions?

Key Challenges and Solutions:

Initial Approach: Initially, Bernadette provided retirees with the government's "Medicare & You" book or directed them to the government website. While this was a good starting point, it often left retirees confused due to the complexity of Medicare.

Overwhelmed with Questions: Despite reading the same material, Bernadette couldn't confidently answer the flood of Medicare-related questions from retirees. This not only created more work for her but also didn't effectively resolve her retirees' healthcare concerns.

Partnering with a Certified Medicare Planner®: By collaborating with a Certified Medicare Planner®, Bernadette can offer her retirees accurate and detailed Medicare information. This partnership ensures that retirees receive expert advice tailored to their individual needs.

Referral to Medicare Experts: For more complex queries, Bernadette can direct retirees to Medicare experts who can guide them through the process, ensuring a smooth transition from employer group healthcare to Medicare.

Providing Accessible Resources: Bernadette can recommend a resource guide, crafted by her team of Certified Medicare Planner® that simplifies Medicare's various parts into understandable sections. This resource can serve as a practical guide for retirees beginning their Medicare journey. We at 123EasyMedicare and American Retirement Advisors are happy to prepare custom guides on demand for corporations; email judi@123EasyMedicare.com to request a consultation with our Executive Relationship Manager.

Summary: To effectively assist her retiring employees, Bernadette can enhance her approach by utilizing the expertise of Medicare professionals and providing accessible, easy-to-understand resources. This strategy not only eases the transition for retirees but also streamlines Bernadette's role in guiding them through their Medicare options.

Janet, an employee at a Fortune 500 company, is nearing her 65th birthday. She is quite satisfied with her current employee health plan and wonders if she should switch to Medicare upon turning 65. She is getting some conflicting information and is debating just signing up for Part A since her HR manger told her it was "free."

Key Steps for Janet:

Check Employer's Medicare Enrollment Policy: Janet's first task is to confirm if her employer requires her to enroll in Medicare at 65. If not, and her current plan is deemed creditable, she can continue with her employer's plan and defer Medicare enrollment without any penalty.

Cost-Benefit Analysis: Janet likes her plan, but it's important to compare the costs and benefits of staying on the employer plan versus switching to Medicare, especially considering potential medical events.

Under Her Employer Plan: If Janet stays with her employer's plan, she'll keep paying her monthly premiums. For a significant medical event, she would first need to meet a $5,000 deductible, then cover various copays and coinsurance, reaching a maximum out-of-pocket cost of $7,350.

Under a Medicare Plan: Switching to Medicare could alter Janet's financial responsibility. Depending on the Medicare plan chosen, her costs for the same medical event could range from as low as $0 to as high as $12,000. This variation is due to different premiums, deductibles, and out-of-pocket limits across Medicare plans.

Considerations for Janet:

Financial Impact: By comparing the financial implications of staying on his employer plan versus transitioning to Medicare, Janet can determine which option is more cost-effective in the event of significant medical needs.

Coverage Quality: Janet should also consider how the benefits and coverage of Medicare plans compare to her current employer plan.

Summary: Before making a decision, Janet should thoroughly analyze both the financial and coverage aspects of her current employer plan and Medicare options. A careful review could potentially save her a significant amount of money, especially in the face of major health events. This is where a "Stay or Go Analysis™" with a Certified Medicare Planner® (CMP) comes in handy. This analysis takes about 45 minutes and is free of charge by a CMP. Best case scenario, you find out that transitioning to Medicare will save you a significant amount of money and offer superior coverage. Worst case scenario, you spend 45 minutes learning about all your Medicare options, and leave knowing that your plan is more appropriate for your needs, no matter what the next salesperson tries to tell you.

Sally, a Benefits Administrator for a small, multi-state company, is often contacted by employees and soon-to-be retirees with questions about Medicare. They are concerned and uncertain about their healthcare options post-retirement. Queries range from concerns about losing employer coverage upon enrolling in Medicare, to confusion over what steps to take to replace their current coverage.

Challenges and Solutions:

Outdated and Incomplete Information: Sally tried to assist with a booklet she created, but keeping it updated was a challenge. Medicare details can change annually, and Sally realized that her booklet, while well-intentioned, was providing outdated and non-compliant information, such as suggesting enrolling in Part A because "it's free."

The Role of HR in Medicare Transition: Employees typically look to their HR department for guidance on healthcare, but HR teams often lack specialized training in Medicare. This can leave retirees without clear direction on how to transition from their employer plan to Medicare.

Key Document for Smooth Transition: One critical tool an employer can provide is an "Employment Verification Form." This form is crucial for the retiree to submit to Medicare, indicating their retirement date and the type of health insurance they had. This helps Medicare determine if there was any lapse in healthcare coverage.

The Importance of Timely Medicare Enrollment: It's essential to note that if individuals over 65 go without a healthcare plan for more than 60 days, they may face lifetime penalties for not enrolling in Medicare when eligible.

Seeking Expert Guidance: For detailed Medicare guidance, consulting with a Certified Medicare Planner® is advisable. They can help avoid mistakes and ensure a smooth transition from employer healthcare to Medicare.

Key Takeaway for Employees:

Consult with HR: Employees should discuss their current benefits with their employer's HR team and obtain the necessary forms for Medicare enrollment.

Expert Assistance: For comprehensive advice, a Certified Medicare Planner® can provide the expertise needed for a successful transition to Medicare.

Summary: While HR departments like Sally's can provide basic guidance and critical documentation, retirees need more comprehensive support for transitioning to Medicare. This scenario emphasizes the importance of seeking expert advice to navigate Medicare's complexities effectively.

Scenario #5:
The Unforeseen Implications of Enrolling in Medicare Part A

Doug, a dedicated employee at a company since 1983 and actively managing his diabetes, is about to turn 65. A colleague advises him to enroll in Medicare Part A since "it's free", and Doug thinks it's a great idea to have extra coverage alongside his employer plan. However, this decision leads to unexpected consequences.

Key Issues and Missteps:

Loss of Manufacturer Discounts: Doug's enrollment in Part A unexpectedly invalidates his manufacturer coupon for insulin, drastically increasing his monthly medication costs. He's surprised to learn that being on Medicare affects his eligibility for certain discounts.

Health Savings Account (HSA) Complications: Doug continues contributing to his HSA, not realizing that enrolling in Medicare Part A disqualifies him from making further contributions. This oversight could lead to tax penalties.

Underestimating Medicare's Impact: The notion of enrolling in "free" Part A without fully understanding its implications led to financial strain for Doug.

What Doug Should Have Done:

Consult a Certified Medicare Planner®: Before enrolling in any part of Medicare, consulting with a Medicare expert would have been crucial. They would have asked Doug specific questions to understand his situation, helping to avoid costly mistakes.

Evaluate Healthcare Needs: A Medicare Planner could have assisted Doug in assessing whether staying on his group plan or transitioning to a comprehensive Medicare plan was more cost-effective, especially considering his medical needs.

Key Takeaway:

Careful Consideration Required: Even though Part A is free, it's important to review the broader implications of enrolling in

Medicare. Timing and personal circumstances play a significant role in making the most out of Medicare plans.

Summary: Doug's scenario highlights the need for careful consideration and expert guidance when making decisions about Medicare enrollment. What seems like a beneficial move at first glance can have unforeseen financial and administrative repercussions.

BONUS
Chapter Eleven:
Questions & Answers

"In the realm of guidance, there are those who lead with the heart to genuinely aid, and those who follow the trail of compensation."

Question **Should I enroll in Medicare if I'm still employed with health benefits?**

Technically there is nothing stopping you from enrolling in Medicare when you turn 65, but if you are already covered on an employer plan, you may not need to. That is why we came up with the Stay or Go Analysis™. We talk about how to complete this analysis in **Chapter 3**. Also, some of the prescription discounts and Health Savings Account contributions you are making might need to stop if you enroll in Part A. See **Chapter 1** for help on making this decision.

https://www.medicare.gov/basics/get-started-with-medicare/medicare-basics/working-past-65

Question **What happens if I don't receive my Medicare card by the time my current health coverage expires?**

Red, white, and blue Medicare cards may take up to six weeks to arrive. Be sure to get an "application summary" from the Social Security office or some other form of proof that you enrolled. This proof will allow your HR department, agent, or advisor to assist you even without the physical card. Not having your physical card shouldn't prevent you from receiving Medicare benefits. You can still access most services by providing your Medicare number to your healthcare providers. And if you have already applied for Medicare, your number will be available via your SSA.gov account.

Question How does payment for Medicare work if I'm not yet collecting Social Security?

Medicare will bill you. You will receive a quarterly invoice from Medicare for the Part B premium (and Part A if you did not have enough eligible quarters earned to qualify to have it premium free.) You can pay online, by mail, or by phone. Here are some additional resources: How to Pay Part A & Part B premiums: https://www.medicare.gov/basics/costs/pay-premiums

Question How does being covered by a spouse's employer insurance affect my Medicare decisions?

It gives you more options! Having creditable coverage through your spouse's employer plan might allow you to delay your enrollment in Medicare without penalty. See **Chapter 1** to see if your spouse's plan will qualify to let you defer your Medicare enrollment.

Question Do I have to sign up for Medicare now that I'm turning 65?

Not necessarily… If you have access to and elect to stay on a creditable employer plan after age 65 and keep working, you do not have to sign up for any part of Medicare. If your employer plan is not deemed creditable, then you will need to enroll in Medicare to avoid a penalty for not enrolling when you were first eligible. See **Chapter 1** for more guidance on what to do when turning 65 and still working.

Question Is Medicare effective on my 65th birthday?

Medicare plans are effective the 1st of the month you turn 65. Exception: If you were born on the first of the month, your Medicare will start the first of the month prior to your birth month. (i.e.: June 1st birthday is eligible to begin Medicare on May 1st) See **Chapter 5 and 6** for details on enrollment.

Question Do I have to get a drug plan if I don't take any prescriptions?

This question is going to depend on who you ask... If you call Medicare, they will tell you that you do not need to enroll in a drug plan... While that is true that it is not required, what they are not telling you, is if you later decide you need/want a drug plan, you will be penalized for every month that you did not have coverage, going all the way back to when you were first eligible. Our recommendation, even if you don't take any medications now, get some sort of Part D so you are covered when you need them without penalty. Check out **Chapters 2 and 3** for help on Part D plans.

Question Can I switch from plan to plan after I'm on Medicare?

Yes, No, Maybe! See **Chapter 6**.

Question With Advantage Plans, does my doctor have to be in the network?

Depends on the plan! HMO plans require you to choose a primary care doctor from the network when you enroll in the plan. That doctor's name will be printed on your card, and they will also be the provider to refer you to 'in-network' specialists for care. The cool thing about 2024, is that most of these HMO plans no longer require you to get a "referral' ahead of time to make sure the plan will pay. You just need to stay in the plan network. (You might still need to supply an 'order' from the referring doctor to make an appointment, however.) Other plan types like PPOs also have a network; however, they have additional out-of-network coverage that essentially lets you go see any doctor you wish, anywhere, so long as that doctor accepts that PPOs payment. See **Chapter 4** for more details.

Question Will my Medicare plan work when I travel?

What do you do when you are traveling in the U.S. or overseas and you need medical care? You will have emergency and urgent care anywhere in the U.S. with a Medicare Advantage Plan, or with a Medigap/Supplement policy. However, Medicare does not work outside the U.S. (Some plans might offer limited coverage outside the country in the form of a reimbursement, but you might be on the hook for expenses you didn't plan for.) We recommend that you get travel insurance when leaving the U.S. for travel. Note: you are covered by Original Medicare in these locations: District of Columbia, Puerto Rico, the U.S. Virgin Islands, Guam, American Samoa, and the Northern Mariana Islands.

`Question` How do Medicare Advantage and Supplement plans differ, and which one should I choose based on my healthcare needs?

See **Chapters 3** and **4**, this is exactly the question these chapters seek to answer for you.

`Question` Are there Medicare plans that include coverage for dental, vision, and other additional benefits similar to Advantage plans?

Medicare covers medical care. Things like dental care, vision care, and other 'extra' coverage you hear about in ads are not options with Medicare. However, many folks choose a Medicare Advantage plan for the additional care and benefits they enjoyed on their former employer plan. **Chapter 3** can help you compare options to determine which plans and benefits are appropriate for you.

Question **How does Medicare work with other specific situations like COBRA?**

COBRA is offered by employers to maintain the health coverage you had when you were employed. However, if you are turning 65 soon or already 65 you must enroll in Parts B and D of Medicare to avoid penalties. If you do not enroll in these parts of Medicare and remain on COBRA instead of Medicare, you will face a lifetime penalty applied to your Part B and D premiums for every month that you did not have this coverage. Even though COBRA is offered by your employer, it is not considered 'creditable', even if on paper it appears to be the exact same coverage you had while working. See **Chapter 1** for more on this.

Question **I have heard that Income Related Monthly Adjustment Amount (IRMAA) is a penalty on your premium for making "too much" money.**

IRMAA is a surcharge amount added to certain income earners plan premiums. Not a penalty. We always joke that Medicare and the IRS are buddies. Medicare assesses any IRMAA surcharges based on your Modified Adjusted Gross Income (MAGI) on your taxes from two years ago. So let us just say you sold your house; that income was reported on your taxes, and that income resulted in a MAGI above the threshold for IRMAA. In two years, you will see a new surcharge on your bill from Medicare... Refer to **Chapter 2** and **Appendix C** for more details.

`Question` How do I manage Medicare alongside an HSA, high deductible health plans, and considerations for noncovered services?

Let's take this in two parts. First, once you enroll in Medicare Part A you must stop your contributions to your HSA (to avoid tax penalties). On the other hand, you can use funds in your HSA account you have accumulated tax-free to pay for qualified medical expenses, such as deductibles, copayments and even premiums for your Medicare Advantage plan, Prescription Drug Plan, and Part B plan. Note: You cannot use it for your Medicare Supplement premium. See **Appendix F** for a chart on this.

`Question` When will I get my Medicare card- I am eligible to apply tomorrow?

If collecting Social Security benefits already, your Medicare card will automagically appear about four months prior to your 65th birthday. If you are not collecting a Social Security benefit yet, you can apply for Medicare three months prior to the month you will turn 65. Your card will arrive in the mail in about 3-6 weeks after your enrollment. You will also be able to check the SSA.gov website to see the status of your enrollment, and if a

Beneficiary ID (Medicare number) was issued, it will provide those details in your SSA.gov portal.

Question If I get Part A for free, why do I need Part B?

Although Part A is free for most folks who qualify for it, the plan only covers medical expenses associated with a hospital stay. What about expenses for preventative care, labs, x-rays, diagnostic tests, and routine doctor visits? What about chronic medical care costs? Those costs can really add up! Having both Parts A and B gives you more coverage like you were used to with your employer plan. Having more coverage helps you avoid many of the costs associated with health changes as we age. See **Chapter 2** that explains the parts of Medicare and why just having Part A is not enough.

Question What if I live in two different places?

Medicare plan eligibility is determined by the primary address on file with Social Security and Medicare. Hundreds of plan combinations are available throughout the country that allow you to 'live' in two different places and maintain access to your chosen providers. The old answer, back when this book was first published, was that "You needed to get a Supplement and a Part D plan" because those are designed to allow you to see any doctor, go to any hospital without referral or issue, anywhere in the USA. In today's market, dozens of Advantage

Plans allow you to leverage national networks too! So you can get care just about anywhere with no issue or loss of coverage just for being somewhere other than your primary residence. That said, you still must pick a plan based on that primary residence, as premiums and eligibility will be based on that primary address.

Question Will Medicare cover massage therapy, physical therapy, hearing aids, or dentures?

Medicare covers many medical procedures and care, but not everything. It is best to refer to Medicare.gov to confirm whether a service, test, or procedure will be covered under Medicare. Since Medicare Advantage plans differ from Original Medicare, your advisor can help you find a plan that might offer partial or full cost for these extra benefits. For a full list of what Medicare itself covers, you can use the following link: https://www.medicare.gov/what-medicare-covers

Question Do I have to re-enroll in my Medicare plan(s) every year?

Not usually…. Medicare Advantage plans, and Prescription Drug Plans will automatically renew/re-enroll you in the same plan so long as the plan still exists in the following year. If either the plan is no longer available, or you stop paying your premiums for either the plan itself and/or Medicare Parts A and

B, then this automatic renewal will not take place. Medicare Supplements renew monthly, and these will also continue indefinitely until either the plan is no longer available, or you stop paying your premiums for the plan. As with life, things change, premiums change, benefits change, and so do your needs. That is why we strongly suggest each-and-every year during the Annual Enrollment Period (See **Chapter 5**) you review your plans, so if a change is needed, you can do so.

Have a question we did not answer?

Email it to

judi@123EasyMedicare.com

or text it to 602-975-0372

with the subject

"Book question"

Appendix A:
Shopper's Guide - Worksheet

	Group Health ins.	Original Medicare	Medicare Supplement	Medicare Advantage
Plan Premium				
Medicare **Part A***				
Medicare **Part B**				
Plan Deductible				
Part A Deductible				
Part B Deductible				
Rx Cost				
Max-out-of-pocket				
Estimated Cost	**High**	You use your plan to its maximum. Meaning you pay your premiums and hit your Maximum-out-of-pocket cost for the year		
	Avg.	You use your plan, see a few doctors, maybe a hospital visit. But nothing major.		
	Low	You take advantage of the "free" services, and just pay your premiums.		

Appendix B:
Medicare Advantage Plan Comparison Chart

1 Physician Name		Plan 1	Plan 2	Plan 3	Plan 4
	PCP				
	PCP				
	Cardio				
	Other				
	Other				
	Other				
2 Hospital					
	Other				
	Other				
3 Prescription Name					
	Dosage	/ day			
4 Preferred Pharmacy					
Alternate Pharmacy					

Appendix C:
Income-Related Monthly Adjustment Amounts (2024)

(Income-Related Monthly Adjustment Amounts)		
https://www.cms.gov/newsroom/fact-sheets/2024-medicare-parts-b-premiums-and-deductibles		
The standard premium for Medicare Part B as of 2024 is $174.70.		
There are contingencies that apply. The following chart explains any additional costs.		
Modified Adjusted Gross Income (MAGI)	**Part B Monthly Cost**	**Part D Monthly Cost**
-Individuals with a MAGI of $103,000 or less -Married Couples with a MAGI of $206,000 or less	Standard Premium Medicare Part B = **$174.70**	Your Medicare Part D Prescription Drug Plan Premium
-Individuals with a MAGI of $103,000 up to $129,000 -Married Couples with a MAGI of $206,000 up to $258,000	Part B Standard Premium + $69.90 = **$244.60**	Your Part D Plan Premium **+ $12.90**
-Individuals with a MAGI of $129,000 up to $161,000 -Married Couples with a MAGI above $258,000 up to $322,000	Part B Standard Premium + $174.70 = **$349.40**	Your Part D Plan Premium **+ $33.80**
-Individuals with a MAGI of $161,000 up to $193,000 -Married Couples with a MAGI above $322,000 up to $386,000	Part B Standard Premium + $279.50 = **$454.20**	Your Part D Plan Premium **+ $53.80**
-Individuals with a MAGI above $193,000 up to $500,000 -Married Couples with a MAGI above $386,000 and $750,000	Part B Standard Premium + $384.30 = **$559.00**	Your Part D Plan Premium **+ $74.20**
-Individuals with a MAGI above $500,000 -Married Couples with a MAGI above $750,000	Part B Standard Premium + $419.30 = **$594.00**	Your Part D Plan Premium **+ $81.00**

Appendix D:
Medigap Plans A-L Comparison Guide

Medigap Plans A Through N

Medigap Plans (Issued after January 1, 2020) — If Medicare eligible after 2019

Medigap policies (including Medicare Select) can only be sold in twelve standardized plans. This chart gives you a quick look at all the Medigap plans and their benefits. Read down to find out what benefits are in each plan. If you need more information call your State Insurance Department.

Benefit	A	B	D	G (High Deductible)	G	K	L	M	N	C* (Only available if you were age 65 before 1/1/2020)	F (High Deductible)	F*
Basic Benefits	Basic Benefits, including 100% Part B co-insurance	Basic Benefits, including 100% Part B co-insurance	Basic Benefits, including 100% Part B co-insurance	Basic Benefits, including 100% Part B co-insurance	Basic Benefits, including 100% Part B co-insurance	Basic Benefits, including 100% Part B co-insurance	Hospital and preventative care paid at 100%; other Benefits paid at 50%	Hospital and preventative care paid at 100%; other Benefits paid at 50%	Basic Benefits, including 100% Part B Co-insurance. You pay up to $20 copay for office visit, up to $50 copay ER	Basic Benefits, Including 100% Part B co-insurance	Basic Benefits, including 100% Part B co-insurance	Basic Benefits, including 100% Part B co-insurance
Skilled Nursing Coinsurance	YOU MUST PAY	YOU MUST PAY	100% Skilled Nursing Coinsurance	100% Skilled Nursing Coinsurance After $2,800 deductible is reached	100% Skilled Nursing Coinsurance	50% Skilled Nursing Coinsurance	75% Skilled Nursing Coinsurance	100% Skilled Nursing Coinsurance	100% Skilled Nursing Coinsurance	100% Skilled Nursing Coinsurance	100% Skilled Nursing After $2,800 deductible is reached	100% Skilled Nursing Coinsurance
Medicare Part A Deductible	YOU MUST PAY	100% Medicare Part A Deductible	100% Medicare Part A Deductible	100% Medicare Part A Deductible After $2,800 deductible is reached	100% Medicare Part A Deductible	50% Medicare Part A Deductible	75% Medicare Part A Deductible	50% Medicare Part A Deductible	100% Medicare Part A Deductible	100% Medicare Part A Deductible	100% Medicare Part A Deductible After $2,800 deductible is reached	100% Medicare Part A Deductible
Medicare Part B Deductible	YOU MUST PAY $240 Annual Medicare Part B Deductible	YOU MUST PAY $240 Annual Medicare Part B Deductible	YOU MUST PAY $240 Annual Medicare Part B Deductible	100% Medicare Part B Deductible After $2,800 deductible is reached	YOU MUST PAY $240 Annual Medicare Part B Deductible	YOU MUST PAY $240 Annual Medicare Part B Deductible	YOU MUST PAY $240 Annual Medicare Part B Deductible	YOU MUST PAY $240 Annual Medicare Part B Deductible	YOU PAY UP TO $20 COPAY FOR OFFICE VISIT, UP TO $50 COPAY ER and $240 Part B Deductible	100% Medicare Part B Deductible	100% Medicare Part B Deductible After $2,800	100% Medicare Part B Deductible
Medicare Part B Excess Charges	NOT COVERED	NOT COVERED	NOT COVERED	100% Medicare Part B Excess Charges After $2,800 deductible is reached	100% Medicare Part B Excess Charges	NOT COVERED	NOT COVERED	NOT COVERED	NOT COVERED	NOT COVERED	100% Medicare Part B Excess Charges After $2,800 deductible is reached	100% Medicare Part B Excess Charges
Foreign Travel Emergency	NOT COVERED	NOT COVERED	80% Foreign Travel Emergency	80% Foreign Travel Emergency After $2,800 deductible is reached	80% Foreign Travel Emergency	NOT COVERED	NOT COVERED	80% Foreign Travel Emergency	80% Foreign Travel Emergency	80% Foreign Travel Emergency	80% Foreign Travel Emergency After $2,800 deductible is reached	80% Foreign Travel Emergency
Out-of-pocket limit						Out-of-pocket limit $7,060; paid at 100% after limit reached	Out-of-pocket limit $3,530; paid at 100% after limit reached					

Medigap Plans C, F and High Deductible are only available if you were age 65 or Medicare eligible before 1/1/2020. Plan N pays 100% of the Part B coinsurance, except for a copayment of up to $20 for some office visits and up to a $50 copayment for emergency room visits that don't result in inpatient admission.

2024 2 MEDIGAP Supplement Plan Compare 01-15-2024

Appendix E
Using Medicare.gov to find plans in your area.

Sourced using www.Medicare.gov.
Images pulled 2/5/2024. Buttons and images might have moved or changed in appearance, but the general flow will likely be similar regardless of when you use this guide.

Medicare has neither reviewed nor endorsed this information. Any information we provide is purely educational based on our experience using Medicare.gov as a publicly available resource.

Step 1:

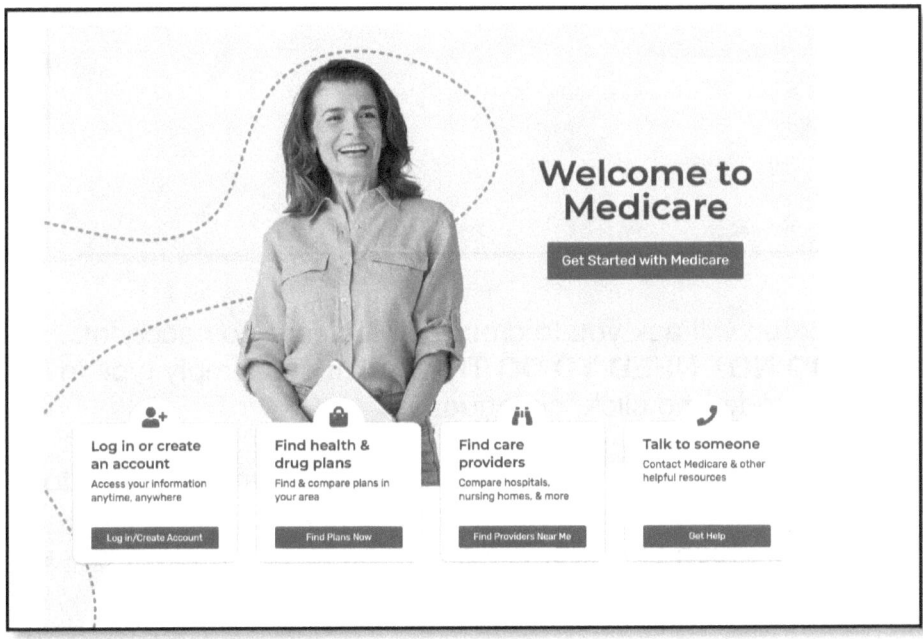

This is the home screen when you go to www.Medicare.gov from here you will have a couple of choices. You will want to find the button that says "Find Plans Now" and click it.

Step 2:

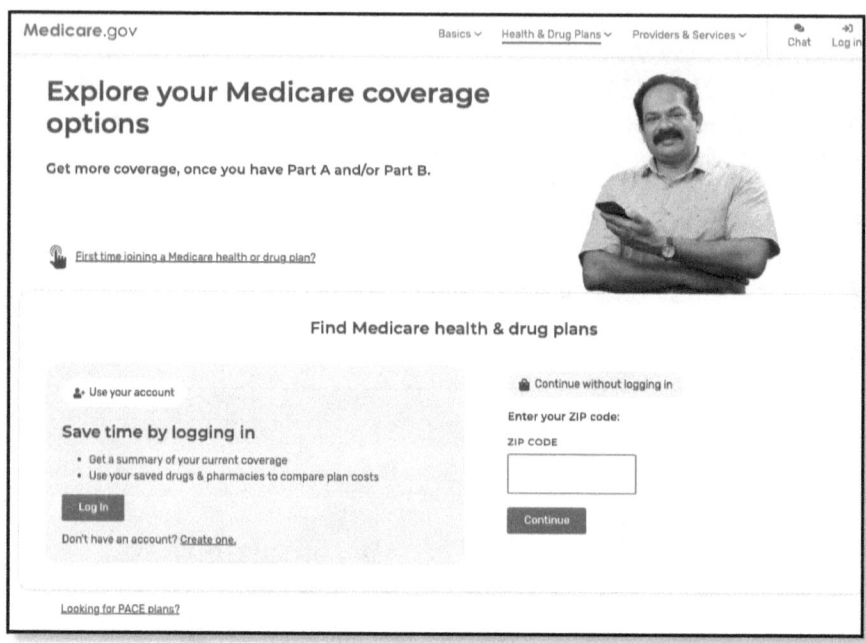

This screen will ask you to create a Medicare.gov account. **YOU DO NOT NEED TO DO THAT.** You can simply type in your zip code and click "continue."

To create an account if you choose to do so, you will need to have your Medicare card number in hand to complete the account creation process. We are going to continue without an account for this example.

Step 3

Next, select the type of plan you want:

◯ Medicare Advantage Plan (Part C)
◯ Medicare drug plan (Part D)
◯ Medigap policy

Which type of plan should I choose? ⓘ

Find Plans   Go Back

After clicking "continue" the same box where you typed in your zip code will change to look like this.

Depending on what you are going into research at the time, you can simply select the box you wish; the following steps and prompts will be virtually identical.

For this example, we are going to select the first choice "Medicare Advantage Plan (Part C) and click "Find Plans."

Step 4

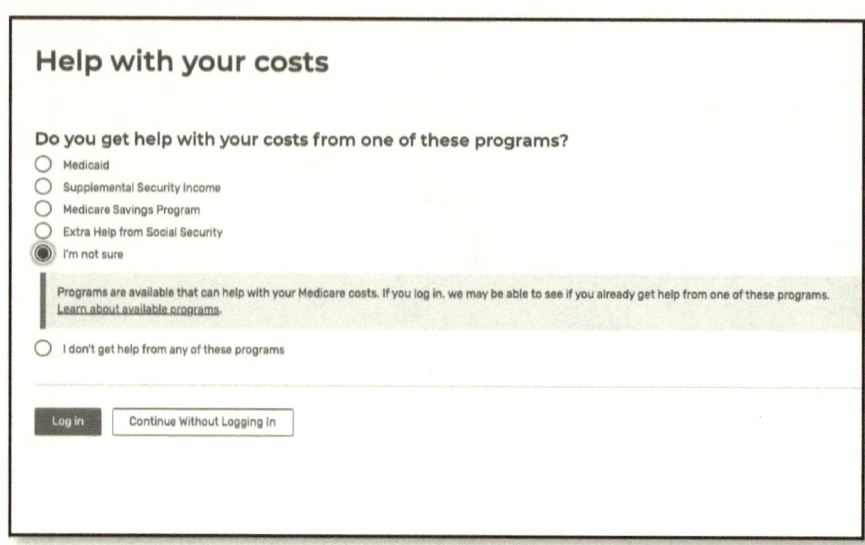

If you do get help from any of these programs go ahead and select which one. Selecting one of these choices will then show you pricing based on your level of extra help. It will also show you plans specifically designed for folks that need the extra help.

For this example, since we want to show EVERY plan, we are going to click "I'm not sure" which will tell the computer not to filter out any results on the final screen. Go ahead and click "Continue without Logging in."

Step 5

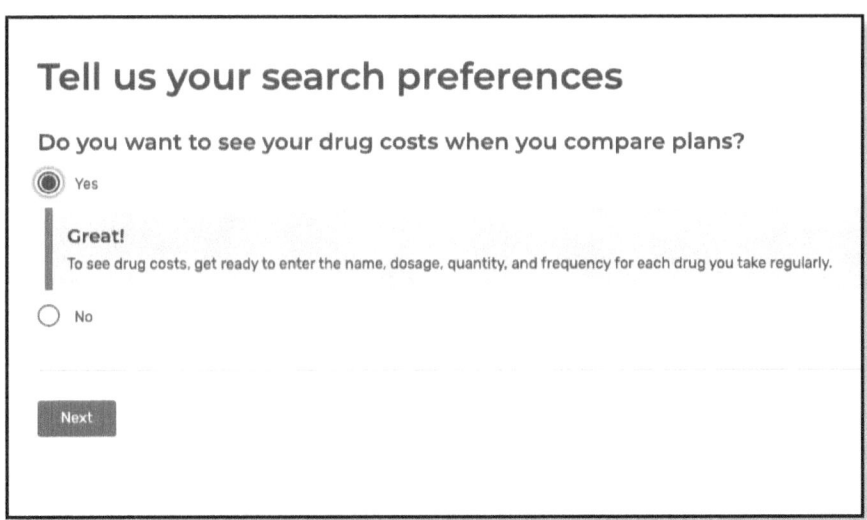

Depending on where you are at in your research process, you may want to go ahead and add the medications that you are taking, so the plan results will populate with the estimated costs of those medications.

If you are at the stage where you are simply searching for what is available, not necessarily what they cost, you can click "No" and then "Next."

For this example, we are going to say "Yes" and enter a couple of generic medications, so you can see what those results look like.

Step 6

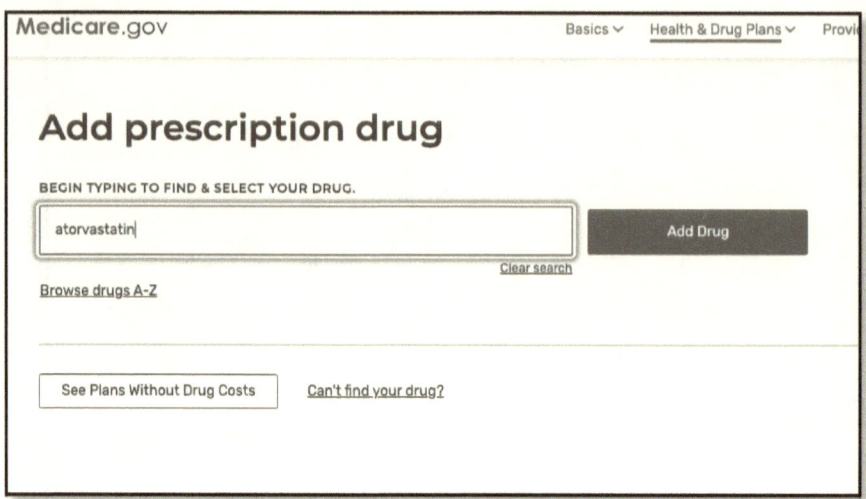

At this point go ahead and enter all the medications that you wish to research. All you need to do is start entering the name of the medication and a drop-down list will appear. Click "Add Drug." The next screen will then ask to enter your dosage information.

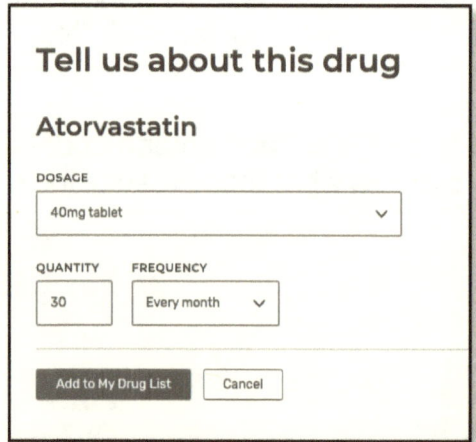

Go ahead and modify as necessary then click "Add to My Drug List." Repeat this step as many times as needed to complete your drug list.

Step 7

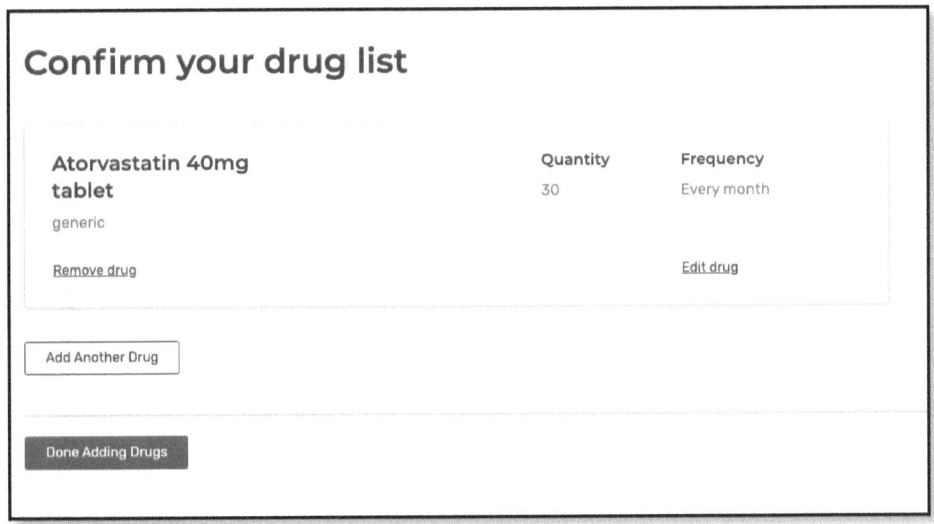

Once you have entered all your Medications click "Done Adding Drugs."

Step 8

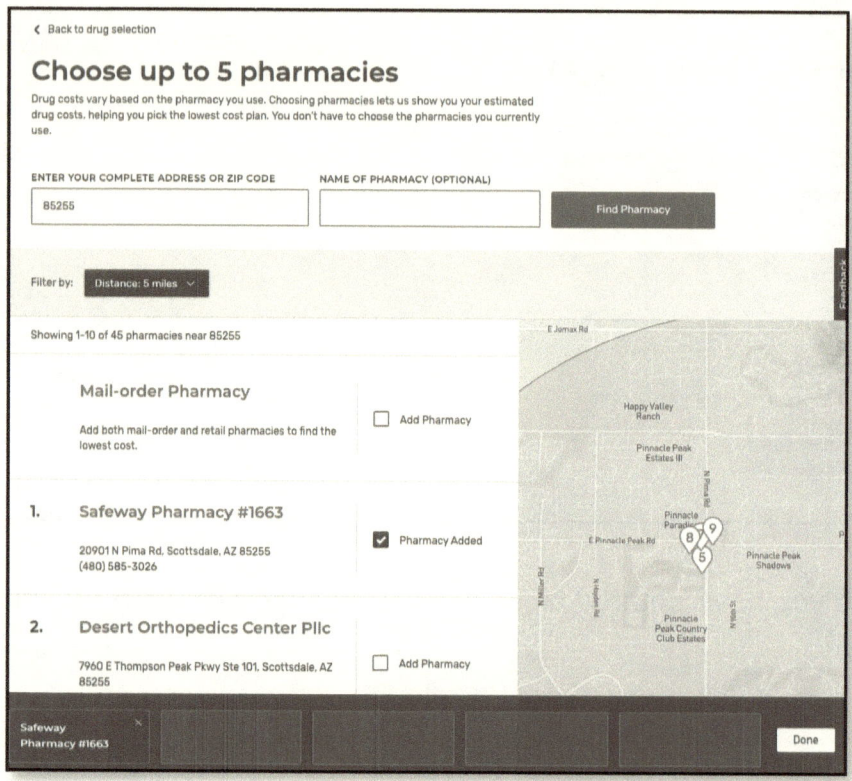

You will then be taken to a screen to add your preferred pharmacy.

It does allow you to add up to 5 different pharmacies.

Important to note that the cost differences will be between the big names, example Walgreens vs CVS, not necessarily between the CVS on the corner by your house, and the CVS down the road.

Once you add your pharmacy, click "Done" on the bottom right of your screen.

Step 9

This is the fun part! Seeing everything that is available!
Here are some tips for navigating all the plans.

1) If you have a chronic condition, like Diabetes, you will
   need to activate the special needs plans, otherwise they
   will not show up in the list.

Make sure to click "Apply" so the list updates.

After this, you are off to the races! The plans will be sorted by
default by "Lowest drug + premium cost."

On this page I will break down some differences to look at between shopping for a Part D plan and an Advantage Plan using Medicare.gov.

When searching for Medicare Advantage Plans.
Medicare.gov is not looking at your providers. It will only consider when sorting the list of options, the cost of your prescription medications and potential premium, if any, for the plan.

Medicare's tool has come a long way in the 20 years we have been using it to help folks; it now includes things like "Plan Benefits." Just please keep in mind, just because a plan "has something like 👀 coverage, it is not saying how much coverage, or even where you must go to use it. So, be careful. If you read this book, you now know how to dig deeper.

When searching for Prescription Drug Plans.
You can simply change the selection at the top under "Plan Type" and all the prescription information will hold, as well as your zip code, so you can continue your research without having to start from the beginning

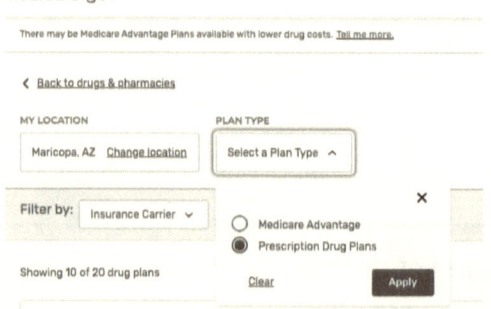

Just be sure to pay attention to the pricing, and at which pharmacy is on by default. Typically, it is the first one you entered.

Appendix F:
What your HSA account can be used for once you enroll in Medicare.

Use of Funds	Allowed
Medicare Part B, Part D, and Advantage Premiums	Yes
Deductibles, Copays, and Coinsurance	Yes
Qualified Medical Expenses (See IRS list):	Doctor visits, urgent care, emergency room services, Hospital stays and surgery, Prescription drugs & over-the-counter medications (with prescription), Dental & vision care (including preventive), Hearing aids, Immunizations, Mental health treatment, Long-term care (limited)
Medigap Premiums	No
Non-qualified Expenses (e.g., gym memberships, cosmetic surgery, non-prescription medications)	No
Contributions after Medicare Enrollment	No

Note: This table provides a summary. Always refer to the IRS website (https://www.irs.gov/forms-pubs/about-publication-969) for a complete list of qualified medical expenses.

References

www.Medicare.gov

www.SSA.gov

www.CMS.gov

www.123EasyMedicare.com

www.AmericanRetire.com

www.123EasyWorkshops.com

www.CertifiedMedicarePlanner.com

www.Medicareatwork.com

Contact a Certified Medicare Planner®

Call: 877-220-1089

Text: 602-975-0372

Email: judi@123EasyMedicare.com

Glossary

Sources: Medicare.gov, Healthcare.gov, CMS.gov, Merriam-Webster.com

Term	Definition
Appeal	Healthcare.gov defines an appeal as a request for your health insurance company or the Health Insurance Marketplace® to review a decision that denies a benefit or payment.
Centers for Medicare and Medicaid Services **(CMS)**	CMS stands for The Centers for Medicare & Medicaid Services and is part of the Department of Health and Human Services (HHS)
Consolidated Omnibus Budget Reconciliation Act **(COBRA)**	Healthcare.gov defines COBA as a federal law that may allow you to keep health coverage after your employment ends temporarily, you lose coverage as a dependent of the covered employee, or another qualifying event. If you elect COBRA (Consolidated Omnibus Budget Reconciliation Act) coverage, you pay 100% of the premiums, including the share the employer used to pay, plus a small administrative fee.
Coinsurance	Healthcare.gov defines it as the percentage of costs of a covered healthcare service you pay (20%, for example) after you've paid your deductible.

Copayment	Healthcare.gov defines it as a fixed amount ($20, for example) you pay for a covered healthcare service after you've paid your deductible.
Deductible	CMS defines a Deductible as the amount you must pay for health care before Medicare begins to pay, either for each benefit period for Part A, or each year for Part B. These amounts can change every year.
Donut Hole	Healthcare.gov defines plans with Medicare prescription drug coverage (Part D) as having a coverage gap (called a "donut hole"). This means that after you and your drug plan have spent a certain amount of money for covered drugs, you have to pay all costs out-of-pocket for your prescriptions up to a yearly limit. Once you have spent up to the yearly limit, your coverage gap ends, and your drug plan helps pay for covered drugs again.
Drug Formulary	CMS defines a Drug Formulary as a list of certain drugs and their proper dosages. In some Medicare health plans, doctors must order or use only drugs listed on the health plan's formulary.
Durable Medical Equipment **(DME)**	CMS defines Durable Medical Equipment (DME) as medical equipment that a doctor orders for use in the home. These items must be reusable, such as walkers, wheelchairs, or hospital beds. DME is paid for under both Medicare Part B and Part A for home health services. It can also be

	purchased or rented items such as hospital beds, iron lungs, oxygen equipment, seat lift equipment, wheelchairs, and other medically necessary equipment prescribed by a health care provider to be used in a patient's home, which Medicare covers.
Evidence of Coverage **(EOC)**	CMS explains that if you're in a Medicare plan, your plan will send you an "Evidence of Coverage" (EOC) each year, usually in the fall. The EOC gives you details about what the plan covers, how much you pay, and more
Guaranteed Issue Rights **(also called "Medigap Protections")**	CMS defines Guaranteed issue rights (also called "Medigap protections") as rights you have in certain situations when insurance companies are required by law to sell or offer you a Medigap policy. In these situations, an insurance company can't deny you a Medigap policy or place conditions on a Medigap policy, like exclusions for pre-existing conditions. It can't charge you more for a Medigap policy because of a past or present health problem.
Hospice Care	CMS defines Hospice as a special way of caring for people who are terminally ill, and for their family. This care includes physical care and counseling. Hospice care is covered under Medicare Part A (Hospital Insurance).

Health Savings Account **(HSA)**	CMS says to avoid a tax penalty, you should stop contributing to your Health Savings Account (HSA) at least 6 months before you apply for Medicare.
Health Maintenance Organization **(HMO)**	A type of health insurance plan that usually limits coverage to care from doctors who work for or contract with the HMO. It generally won't cover out-of-network care except in an emergency. An HMO may require you to live or work in its service area to be eligible for coverage. HMOs often provide integrated care and focus on prevention and wellness.
Initial Enrollment Period **(IEP)**	CMS defines IEP or The Initial Enrollment Period as the first chance you have to enroll in Medicare Part B. Your Initial Enrollment Period starts three months before you first meet all the eligibility requirements for Medicare and lasts for seven months. When you're first eligible for Medicare, you have a 7-month Initial Enrollment Period to sign up for Part A and/or Part B. If you're eligible for Medicare when you turn 65, you can sign up during the 7-month period that begins 3 months before the month you turn 65. Including the month you turn 65.
Income Related Monthly Adjustment Amount	CMS explains that if your modified adjusted gross income is above a certain amount, you may pay an Income Related Monthly Adjustment Amount (IRMAA). Medicare uses the modified adjusted gross income reported on your IRS tax return from 2

(IRMAA)	years ago. This is the most recent tax return information provided to Social Security by the IRS.
Long-Term Care	Services that include medical and non-medical care are provided to people who cannot perform basic activities of daily living, such as dressing or bathing. Long-term support and services can be provided at home, in the community, in assisted living, or in nursing homes. Individuals may need long-term support and services at any age. Medicare and most health insurance plans don't pay for long-term care.
Maximum Out- of-Pocket **(MOOP)**	CMS defines the maximum out-of-pocket as the beneficiary's maximum dollar liability amount for a specified period.
Medicaid	CMS defines Medicaid as a joint federal and state program that helps with medical costs for some people with low incomes and limited resources. Medicaid programs vary from state to state, but most healthcare costs are covered if you qualify for both Medicare and Medicaid.
Medicare	Per CMS, Medicare provides health insurance coverage to individuals aged 65 and over, those under age 65 with certain disabilities, and individuals of all ages with ESRD. Medicaid provides medical benefits to groups of low-income people, some of whom may have no medical insurance or inadequate medical insurance.

Medicare Health Maintenance Organization **(HMO)**	CMS defines a Medicare Health Maintenance Organization (HMO) Plan as a type of Medicare managed care plan where a group of doctors, hospitals, and other healthcare providers agree to give health care to Medicare beneficiaries for a set amount of money from Medicare every month. You usually must get your care from the providers in the plan.
Medicare Part A **(Hospital Insurance)**	CMS states that Medicare Part A covers inpatient hospital stays, care in a skilled nursing facility, hospice care, and some home health care.
Medicare Part B **(Medical Services)**	CMS defines Medicare Part B as Medicare medical insurance that helps pay for doctor's services, outpatient hospital care, durable medical equipment, and some medical services that aren't covered by Part A.
Medicare Advantage Plan **(Part C)**	CMS says that Medicare Advantage Plans are another way to get your Medicare Part A and Part B coverage. Medicare Advantage Plans, sometimes called "Part C" or "MA Plans," are offered by Medicare-approved private companies that must follow rules set by Medicare. Most Medicare Advantage Plans include drug coverage (Part D).
Medicare Part D	CMS defines Medicare Drug Coverage and Plan Part D as optional benefits for prescription drugs available to all people with Medicare for an additional charge. This

(Prescription Drug Plan)	coverage is offered by insurance companies and other private companies and is approved by Medicare.
Medicare Preferred Provider Organization **(PPO)**	CMS defines a Medicare Preferred Provider Organization (PPO) Plan as a type of Medicare Advantage Plan in which you use doctors, hospitals, and providers that belong to the network. You can use doctors, hospitals, and providers outside of the network for an additional cost.
Medicare Medical Savings Account **(MSA)**	CMS defines MSA Plans as combining a high-deductible Medicare Advantage Plan and a bank account. The plan deposits money from Medicare into the account. You can use the money in this account to pay for your healthcare costs, but only Medicare-covered expenses count toward your deductible. The amount deposited is usually less than your deductible amount, so you will generally have to pay out-of-pocket before your coverage begins.
Medicare Savings Program	CMS says a Medicare Savings Program is a Medicaid program that helps people with limited income and resources pay some or all of their Medicare premiums, deductibles, and coinsurance.
Medigap Policy **(Medicare Supplement)**	CMS defines a Medigap policy / Medicare Supplement as a supplement insurance policy sold by private insurance companies to fill "gaps" in Original Medicare Plan coverage. Except in Massachusetts,

	Minnesota, and Wisconsin, there are 10 standardized plans labeled Plan A through Plan J. Medigap policies only work with the Original Medicare Plan.
Network Plan	Healthcare.gov defines this as a health plan that contracts with doctors, hospitals, pharmacies, and other healthcare providers to provide members of the plan with services and supplies at a discounted price.
Open Enrollment Period **(OEP)**	CMS defines the Medicare Advantage Open Enrollment Period as a period from January 1 – March 31 each year. If you're enrolled in a Medicare Advantage Plan, you can switch to a different Medicare Advantage Plan or switch to Original Medicare (and join a separate Medicare drug plan) once during this time.
Original Medicare	**CMS defines** Original Medicare as a fee-for-service health plan with two parts: Part A (Hospital Insurance) and Part B (Medical Insurance). After you pay a deductible, Medicare pays its share of the Medicare-approved amount, and you pay your share (coinsurance and deductibles).
Over-the-Counter Drug	An over-the-counter drug is a drug that you can buy without a prescription at your local pharmacy or drug store. These drugs are not covered by Medicare Part D.
Pharmacy	A place where medicines are compounded or dispensed. (Merriam-Webster)

Primary Care Physician **(PCP)**	CMS explains that a Primary Care Doctor/Physician is a doctor who is trained to give you basic care. Your primary care doctor is the doctor you see first for most health problems. He or she makes sure that you get the care that you need to keep you healthy. He or she also may talk with other doctors and health care providers about your care and refer you to them. In many Medicare-managed care plans, you must see your primary care doctor before seeing any other health care provider.
Premium	CMS defines a Premium as the periodic payment to Medicare, an insurance company, or a health care plan for health or prescription drug coverage.
Skilled Nursing Care	Healthcare.gov says these are services from licensed nurses in your own home or a nursing home. Technicians and therapists provide skilled care services in your own home or in a nursing home.
Special Enrollment Period **(SEP)**	CMS defines a Special Enrollment Period (SEP) as a set time when you can sign up for Medicare Part B if you didn't take Medicare Part B during the Initial Enrollment Period because you or your spouse were working and had group health plan coverage through the employer or union. You can sign up anytime you are covered under the group plan based on your current employment status. The last eight months of the Special Enrollment Period starts the month after the

	employment ends or the group health coverage ends, whichever comes first.
TRICARE	Healthcare.gov says this is a healthcare program for active-duty and retired uniformed service members and their families.
Zoo	Just to see if anyone was reading this far... Google defines this as "a situation characterized by confusion and disorder."

Index

About the Authors

Ian M. Schaeffer

As a seasoned Industrial Engineer with a drive and a passion to make things more efficient, Mr. Schaeffer knows something about wrapping his arms around large, multi-faceted projects and breaking them down into process-driven, manageable tasks.

His experience ranges from designing six-sigma process control systems on the manufacturing floor to implementing lean principles, improving data flow, and effective cross and departmental communication in the insurance and wealth management space.

Mr. Schaeffer capitalizes on his problem-solving and efficiency designs by acting as the organizational backbone and corporate strategist for parent company American Retirement Advisors as their Chief Operating Officer. He is also the CEO of his start-up consulting firm, The Medicare Architects, whose team helps Benefits and Human Resources partners easily and seamlessly transition retiring employees to Medicare. Besides writing, public speaking, expanding the cartoon presence of his senior advocate "Easy Eddie," and helping clients achieve their retirement goals, Mr. Schaeffer also collects rare history books, enjoys adventuring backroads, and explores New England with his wife, Elise, and daughter, Maddie.

David P. Schaeffer

David Schaeffer's career spanning over two decades stands as a testament to his dedication to simplifying Medicare for retirees from renowned organizations like IBM, Pitney Bowes, Honeywell, Raytheon, Banner Healthcare, and so many more.

His insights, featured in "The American Retirement Advisor," illuminate changes in the Medicare and retirement planning space offering invaluable guidance to thousands of retirees nationwide. As the brain behind 123EasyMedicare.com, David democratizes the process of comparing Medicare plans, by providing unbiased, unfiltered information through his free "Medicare Made 123 Easy" Workshops.

His work extends to creating the nation's first federally protected distinction, "Certified Medicare Planner®." This pioneering achievement marks a significant milestone in the industry, establishing a benchmark of trust and excellence within the community. His efforts underscore a deep commitment to not only safeguarding but also enhancing the integrity of Medicare advisory services. Beyond his professional achievements, being featured in Forbes, and Inc. Magazine, David serves as a consultant to major insurance carriers, advocating for the thousands of clients he represents and fostering a transparent Medicare ecosystem. Outside of his office setting, David lives in Cave Creek pursuing his passion of preparing for the unexpected and overlanding in his Jeep with his beautiful wife, Thea, and office dog, Rex.

SOCIAL MEDIA

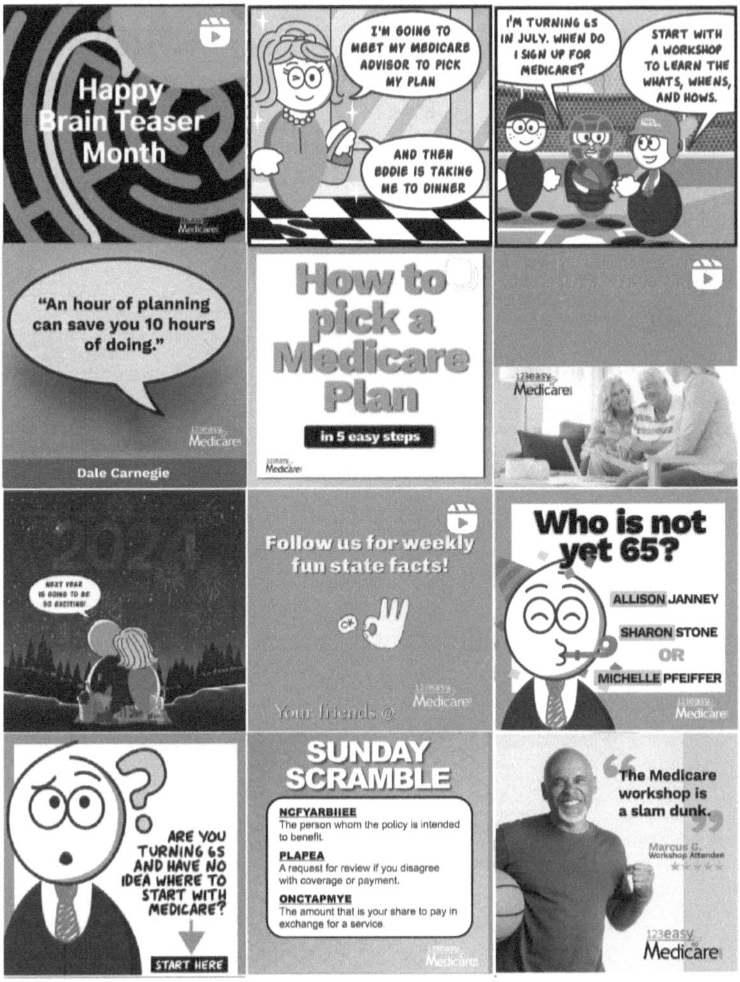

Follow us on your favorite sites: Facebook, Instagram, or YouTube. Gain insights on all things Medicare, including testimonials and of course, Easy Eddie cartoons!

NEWSLETTER

**Stay connected with your FREE subscription to
<u>The American Retirement Advisor</u> newsletter.
A monthy newsletter to keep you informed and edutained!**